LITTLE MISS MERIT BADGE

MEMOIR

BY RONDA BEAMAN

Make merit,
Ronda

Dedication

For Lander, Kili, Jet, and anyone else
who may call me Go-Go.

*Man never made any material as resilient
as the human spirit.*

— BERN WILLIAMS

*I know of no such unquestionable badge and ensign
of a sovereign mind as that of tenacity of purpose ...*

— RALPH WALDO EMERSON

NOTE TO READER:
With this book I have finally 'fessed up. I have freely and universally admitted my lies, falsehoods, whoppers, and tall tales. Anything in my memoir that rings untrue, is at odds with what family members, friends, or history recalls is not due to a lack of character or an aversion to veracity. Please attribute any errors in chronology, titles, names, or judgment to age, typos, or simple storyteller embellishment.

Wyatt-MacKenzie Publishing
DEADWOOD, OREGON

Little Miss Merit Badge: A Memoir
by Ronda Beaman

ISBN: 978-1-936214-47-1
Library of Congress Control Number: 2011940736

Wyatt-MacKenzie Publishing, Inc, Deadwood, Oregon
www.WyattMacKenzie.com

Note about photographs of the author's badges in each chapter:
The official badges are owned by Girl Scouts of the USA and used by permission.
The GIRL SCOUTS® name, mark and all associated trademarks
and logotypes are owned by Girl Scouts of the USA.

Author photo by David Lawrence.

Contact the author at:
www.LittleMissMeritBadge.com

Contents

Girl Scout Law   1

Introduction
The Motto: Be Prepared   3

BADGE One
Write All About It   7

BADGE Two
My Heritage   17

BADGE Three
On My Way   31

BADGE Four
Making Music   49

BADGE Five
Dance Badge   75

BADGE Six
Math Whiz   93

BADGE Seven
The Cookie Connection   117

BADGE Eight
Healthy Relationships   137

BADGE Nine
Creative Solutions   163

BADGE Ten
Water Fun   179

BADGE Eleven
Becoming A Teenager   195

BADGE Twelve
Being My Best   215

Epilogue
The Journey Award   223

Acknowledgements   229

Book Club Questions   231

About the Author   233

Girl Scout Law (1963)

1. A Girl Scout's honor is to be trusted.

2. A Girl Scout is loyal.

3. A Girl Scout's duty is to be useful; and to help others.

4. A Girl Scout is a friend to all and a sister to every Girl Scout.

5. A Girl Scout is courteous.

6. A Girl Scout is a friend to animals.

7. A Girl Scout obeys orders.

8. A Girl Scout is cheerful.

9. A Girl Scout is thrifty.

10. A Girl Scout is clean in thought, word, and deed.

Introduction

~⊚~

The Motto: Be Prepared

I am singing a Beatles song in the emergency room.

I am behind a green curtain that separates me from a woman screaming in Spanish and a shooting victim just brought in on a stretcher. I can't see anything, but blood is rivering it's way toward my feet.

"Sing 'Rocky Raccoon' to him, Ronda. Maybe he'll hear you, maybe he'll wake up," my mother pleads. It is one of the songs my sister and I used to sing from the backseat on interminable car trips through the desert.

I maneuver my way past the wrangle of life-support machinery and start belting out the silly number my father loved. I sing strongly and off key. I have to compete with the pumping accordion cacophony of the rubber heart and the whirring of the many machines that keep his body functioning.

*"Now somewhere in the black mountain hills of Dakota
There lived a young boy named Rocky Raccoon ..."*

I study his profile as I sing, cognizant of the drama unfolding around me. He is seventy-four years old and will die at any moment from the Stage Four lung cancer diagnosed three months earlier. Here in the hospital he is slowly deflating, like a basketball left too long in the garage.

When my mother called with the bad news, she told us—his three adult children—not to mention the diagnosis to him, to just act as if he "has a cold." She asked that we pretend everything was all right. We were all pretty good at pretending, but no one could top him. He didn't quit his job. He never talked about being sick. There were no last loving words shared with any of us, no regrets expressed, or amends made.

Last night, just one hour after his second chemotherapy treatment, he played tennis. Covered with radiation burns and sweating toxic chemicals, he served, lobbed, and smashed the ball for over two hours. He played a full two-set match—and won. It was almost as though he believed that if he just played hard enough, he could even beat cancer with his racket.

"And one day his woman ran off with another guy ..."

As I continue the song, my father's hands begin a rhythmic twitching, it is the first time he has shown any signs of life since he was thrown in an ambulance almost six hours ago.

He had gotten up this morning, told my mother he felt cold and weak, but he would not consider staying home from work. It was this ethic that had allowed him at one time to be a bank president, vice-president of a major corporation, and own car dealerships, all without the benefit of a college education. That was long ago and far away, and he had since lost most everything he had ever gained.

On this day, he ate his daily oatmeal, grabbed the car keys and headed to his minimum wage job doing the books for a plastering business. He collapsed at his office and the next time my mother saw him was here, in the hospital, with all of his organs shut down from septic shock.

Once a man who looked like a celebrity—I was often with him when people would mistake him for Johnny Carson—he now looks like the dehydrated, colorless, and prickly towns he has lived in for the past forty years. The doctors say he will die from the cancer, but I believe it's malignant hate and anger that will kill him.

> *"He hit young Rocky in the eye*
> *Rocky didn't like that he said I'm gonna get that boy ..."*

His entire body is now flailing and flopping on the gurney. His frenzied limbs are akimbo, like an old worn puppet with an amateur working the strings. My mother is holding his hand and becoming anxious and agitated the more he moves. I keep singing, looking briefly into her eyes and see her fear and confusion.

It still amazes me that my parents stayed married for fifty-five years, through over fifty moves, dozens of jobs, adultery, and incessant acrimony. The price paid for this union by their three now-adult children includes eight marriages, nine grandchildren, alcoholism, substance abuse, eating disorders, domestic violence, and a blistering emptiness in the place of a warm familial hearth making even small talk between us onerous and painful.

> *"So one day he walked into town*
> *Booked himself a room in the local saloon*
> *Rocky Raccoon checked into his room ..."*

My mother yells, "Stop singing! You are bothering him, Ronda. Stop singing, stop now!" She cries and collapses across his body, holding him down and sobbing into his chest. His eyes are still shut, the machines are still fighting for him, but with her embrace and my silence, he calms immediately.

I have to hand it to my father—even in a coma he can still deliver a bad review, I think smiling wryly.

After all these years, I knew the truth. It's not that my mother was wrong. Oh, I was bothering him, alright. I can even say with confidence that he heard my singing and was obviously moved by me.

But, as usual, he just didn't think I was any good.

At anything.

On the bright side, growing up with a father who wanted me to shut up and go away taught me to always Be Prepared.

Memoirs are people's written memories of their lives.
Try your hand at writing a memoir. Make your story have a
point. Why should someone want to read it?

GIRL SCOUT BADGE BOOK

Write All About It

I am gulping green Kool-Aid and stuffing gold Lorne Doone cookies into my mouth, but I feel no benefit from the sugar high. I am into the tough stuff.

I'm only six and I am already hooked.

This drug gives me the strength of a super hero and the courage to have convictions. It colors my otherwise dull world and satisfies both a gnawing hunger for acceptance and a seemingly endless craving for acknowledgement.

Many decades and hundreds of mistakes later, I can still name the place, the time, and the moment my habit took hold. **Phoenix, Arizona. September, 1960. 7 p.m. The pusher?** One Mrs. Delores Frietas, the leader of the Cactus-Pine Council Girl Scout Troop 1062.

It is a long, hot walk to our first troop meeting. After reading street signs and looking both ways in the crosswalks, I finally stumble into her home, capped in my orange and brown beanie, bobby-pinned at what I consider a jaunty angle. I am there despite the fact that my father complains that "Brownie" is a stupid name. He suggests I join the Campfire Girls instead, because "Bluebird" not only sounds nicer, the light blue uniforms look "a helluva lot" better. But I have gone ahead and signed on with the Brownies, and because I have done this, he refuses to give me a lift the twelve blocks it takes me to get to the scene of the crime.

"Find your own way," he says, not for the first or last time in my life.

I join a flock of other young, impressionable users in light brown uniforms, staggering out of the desert heat and into the swamp cooled home and open arms of our gang leader. With a practiced flourish reminiscent of state fair carnies who are trying to entice you to choose their arcade game, she waves us into the rumpus room. She then points us toward the sliding glass doors and out into a small backyard landscaped in popular Phoenician style—desert rocks and cactus. In addition to the brightly painted, plaster of Paris donkey planted unlife-like in gravel, there are six fiery tiki torches guiding our way toward a concrete wall festooned with Girl Scout posters urging us to have "Character, Courage, and Conviction," as well as "Be a Super Scout, Sell a Cookie!"

Plump and permanently moist above her lips and under her eyes, Troop Leader Frietas hands each of us a name tag followed by a two fingered salute. She urges us to "Mix and Mingle" but none of us knows what that means so we all just stand around feigning interest in a fake donkey while shoving cookies in our mouths.

She should have made brownies to serve to the Brownies, I think. Ha-ha ... brownies for Brownies. I mean, how tough is that?

The meeting is officially called to order, following a lively Mariachi-type rendition by Mrs. Frietas of "La Cucaracha." She even shakes marimbas and tosses her "Souvenir from Nogales" sombrero into the crowd of dazzled Brownies. Only in the southwest does a cockroach get his own song and dance.

All in attendance are mightily impressed, as gauged by the fact that most of us quit chewing our cookies and applaud heartily as she finishes. The evening was turning into a bona fide special event, like going to a Saturday matinee and then getting candy too!

Breathless after her spry dance, Mrs. Frietas puffily introduces a guest speaker, a First Class Girl Scout named Jolene, who, the troop leader swoons, "Started her scouting adventure sitting where you are tonight. Jolene was a little Brownie, like you girls, and her first meeting was in my home, just like yours is." They hold hands and beam at us proudly, holding the pose until one of my fellow Brownies chums figures out we are suppose to applaud again.

So, we do. Wildly, fueled now by sugar, and being young girls on the verge ... of something.

Jolene, on the face of it, doesn't look exceptional; she is a pimply teen with a big-toothed smile and perfectly-flipped-and-hair-sprayed dishwater blonde hair. But as she saunters to the center of the rocky yard, my eyes are drawn down from her face to her chest. What I see makes me drop my Kool-Aid, spill my cookies, and stare, googly-eyed and slack-jawed ...

I see ...

Badges. Badges and badges.

And more badges.

Little, round patches—each with a secret symbol embroidered in the center—are sewn on to a dark green sash that Jolene wears with the posture and pride of a hometown beauty queen.

Jolene clears her throat politely, explaining to us how she's earned the badges and how becoming a Girl Scout has given her confidence and a great feeling of belonging. My eyes glaze and my heart races as I picture myself tra-la-laing down a green and yellow brick road with a full sash and perfect hair. Thanks to Jolene, I begin to see myself on a road paved with badges that can possibly—hopefully—take me far from home and away from my family. A road I feel sure will be toward a bigger and better version of who I might become.

Jolene keeps talking and I can feel myself turning into Snidely Whiplash, the cartoon villain, as I wring my hands together, plotting to become Queen of the Badges. I can earn more than Jolene, more than Mrs. Frietas, more, ... more than anyone.

I look menacingly at my peers, scratch that, my competitors and think, *Mwa-ha-ha-haaaa!* If I had a moustache I would twirl it.

This is my destiny. I feel high as I define my dream and my direction toward being somebody valuable and important, a Super Scout.

I stride home that night with a newfound—actually a first found—sense of purpose coupled with a slight badge hoarding disorder.

I am practically floating through our carport, swooshing past our electric blue, rag top, Dreamily, I open the aluminum screen door that leads to our avocado and bronze colored kitchen. I glance at the dancing carrots on the cafe curtains hanging crisply in the kitchen window and feel a kinship with their eager, rumba-ing, smiling, colorfulness.

Inside my house I am instantly peeled and shredded by the tossed salad of my real world. My grandmother is in the living room, dancing topless with her size forty-four "woo-woos" bouncing to the beat of Elvis blasting from the stereo. My mother is waving a worn tea towel, yelling at her to at least put on a bra. My younger brother and sister are huddled in the hallway crying about Dusty, the beagle we got from the pound. Between sobs I am able to figure out that my father took Dusty out to the desert that day and left him to "live with the coyotes," because Dusty ate a neighbor's pigeon. *What kind of kook owns a pet pigeon anyway?* I wonder, feeling bad for my siblings and worse for the dog.

Amidst all the hullabaloo, there is my father, who takes one look at me, my beanie in my hand, the new uniform now wilted from the heat, my official Brownie belt and coin purse askew from the hike home, and then blows cigarette smoke my way saying, "Welcome back there, Miss Brownie. You look like a walking dirt clod." He flicks ash from his Tareyton on both my shoulders and laughs, "There, now you're a decorated scout, I made you a general."

As I brush off the ash with as much dignity as a six-year-old can muster I think, can I put myself up for adoption?

During my formative years in the Girl Scouts, I eventually earned so many merit badges that I had to wear two sashes to hold them all. Dressed in my uniform and anchored to the earth by my gaggle of pins, ribbons, awards, and patrol leader cords, I looked like the Barbie doll version of General Patton. And it didn't stop there. For most of my life, if there was an award to be won, an honor to be earned, an office to run for, or a competition to enter, I would—invariably, almost manically—become a contender, raise my hand, or jump right in.

My first badge attempt was keeping a diary to earn the Write All About It badge.

I lied on every page.

I like to think of my fiction as early signs of creativity. With shear pluck and perspicacity I wrote about the life I wanted, rather than the life I had. I confided to my diary the details of whom and what I hoped to be, using my pencil like a fairy godmother uses her magic wand, unreasonably hoping some of the stories and wishes might come true. Even though it says Jimmy Boerner—the cutest boy in eighth grade—kissed fifth grade me in the dugout after the Little League championship game, it never happened. As for being the state Olympian in the hop-skip-jump in third grade? False. Created the best painting of Egyptian pyramids in my second grade class, so "early signs of gifted in it's use of colors and perspective" it was going to hang in Principal Bonaco's office? This was an artistic lie.

I was never the fastest runner, smartest student, or prettiest girl, no lie. Determined, over-achieving, and diligent? Sure. Great imagination? You should read my diary.

I really wanted to be gifted. Sadly, pretending I had a gift or skill wasn't ingenious, it just made me an imposter. I spent a lot of ungifted brain space wondering, if a person *is* gifted, do they want to be normal? I would trade, I thought. Give me forte, world; choose me as a prodigy and then stand back. I knew I could handle it.

And famous. I had a prodigious appetite for fame. I wanted Annette's slot on the *Mickey Mouse Club*, or to be Penny on the *Sky King Show*. My family had assured me over and over again that I was not endowed with the good looks or talent for this line of work, so I resourcefully documented far-fetched adventures that allowed me—for a few moments every night before bed as I wrote large—to be who, where, and what I wanted to be.

There are whole episodes of foreign travel I describe in detail, even though the most foreign thing I did while growing up was eat Mexican food. If I had as many friends clamoring for my attention as I said I had, there would never have been time to write in my diary. Although I never lived in the same house for longer than three years—and attended three first grades, four different elementary schools, and three freshman classes in high school, eventually moving thirty-five times before high school was over—the house and family I describe in diary-detail was lifted directly from my favorite television program, the *Donna Reed Show*. I actually gave my mother a string of plastic pop-bead pearls one Mother's Day, hoping she would wear them, like Donna, while she vacuumed. I told my diary that "Help Me, Rhonda" by the Beach Boys was written for me after meeting all of them at a swim party and talking to Denny, the cute drummer, who fell in love with me under the flame of a flickering Bug-B-Gone lamp. The real song written for me should have been, "Liar, Liar, Pants on Fire."

In my diary delusions I won every school election, got the highest test scores, was always asked to dance, and got the lead in every play. I never had a pimple or a problem.

Contrary to what I wrote in my red leather, open-only-by-hidden-gold-key diary, I did not grow up to be a President, a Premier, or a Princess. Truthfully, I never worked the streets at night and then became a nun, I was never left for dead on the top of a snow capped mountain, or sold into child slavery.

I did not chew off any of my body parts, drink or eat myself into a fatal condition, and I am not related to anyone famous or infamous. I am not even an ordinary person who thinks they have lived an extraordinary life. But I have—and for no apparent reason—always have had, a resilient sense of specialness, regardless of the fact that I grew up with someone who did anything he could to keep me from developing even the minimal amount of self-esteem.

In writing my diary, I certainly didn't consciously intend to break the first rule of a good Girl Scout, which is to be truthful and trustworthy at all times. Even as a child I had an inkling that life becomes the stories that we weave and I honestly-fervently hoped and believed that if I could create an interesting, funny, popular person on paper, I might actually become her. I perpetrated a "Life-Lie" which is "the necessary delusion that makes life possible, gives us hope, even if it's unreasonable hope."

I lacked the emotional vocabulary to describe the fact that I was living in a ramshackle series of houses with two childish parents who never explained why we were moving again, who thought nothing of making us change schools midyear, multiple times (even if we were moving within the same town), who made us forego classes or activities or friendships or commitments—and offered us very little in return.

It was the Girl Scouts—the troop leaders, the members, and the organization's ideals—who gave my unquenchable hope a direction and provided me a pledge that I needed, heeded, and good deeded to build my life story.

So, at last, this is the *true* account of how and why I over-abundantly, desperately, ridiculously, sometimes dishonestly, and often comically discovered that if you fulfill the requirements, a life of merit can be the reward for those who try their best to do their duty ... and try, and try, and try ...

Your heritage is made up of ... your family traditions and values. What have you inherited that makes you the person you are?

GIRL SCOUT BADGE BOOK

My Heritage

It is 11:59 a.m., the wind is howling, rain is cascading down the hospital window, and I am born to Gidget and Moon Doggie who, mercifully, decide not to name me Sunny.

My parents met at a California beach during high school and though they weren't named Gidget or Moon Doggie, that's who they thought they were—young, golden, beautiful teenagers with a beckoning horizon and calm sea ahead of them.

My father was the captain of the basketball team and my mother was a dancing, singing, local child star who'd never made it to the big time. They clinched their union—and my birth date—in the backseat of my father's Oldsmobile coup on the night of senior prom.

My father was a very handsome, chiseled, blue-eyed, gleaming teeth like Chiclets gum kinda guy. He was like Frankie Avalon and Fabian all rolled into one. He wore his collars turned up, slicked back his hair, and dyed his blue jeans orange. As an only child his mother treated him like a prince, practically giving him a standing ovation every time he entered the kitchen for breakfast.

The co-eds of Mark Keppel High in Alhambra, California, actually created an honest to goodness fan club in his honor. The club had a thriving membership, collected dues, and held monthly meetings. Every now and then my father would grace them with his presence at the meetings and autograph the 5x7 glossies of his latest free throw or jump shot that had been taken for the school newspaper.

My mother was just sixteen when they met. She was petite, auburn haired, and a dead ringer for Debbie Reynolds. What she may have lacked in nobility in her home, she made up for with her regal bearing. Her report cards from the time she entered first grade until she finished high school consistently included remarks from her teachers that confirmed that my mother "thinks she knows everything," is "not inclined to listen or take direction," and "remains aloof from, and thinks she's better than the other students."

She was living with her mother and her step-father, a former semi-pro baseball player who last name was Homer.

Really.

He spent most of his time trying to score with his step-daughters. By the time she met my father she was ready for a new man in her life. Not only was she tired of avoiding Homer's pitches, she was also tired of babysitting—virtually raising—her half-brother, who was ten years younger than she.

My mother signed up for my father's fan club and got me as a membership bonus. They eloped right after high school graduation. This did not stop my father from accepting a basketball scholarship to Kansas State University. He left my mother living with her mother in California. He was probably playing hoops at KSU on the wintery, February night I was born.

While my father was pledging a fraternity and enjoying being the "Big Man on Campus," my mother worked at the local phone company right up until she went into labor with me. She couldn't wait until her husband, the real operator, would come home to his "girls" when his freshman year ended in June. Until then, my grandmother—who was all of thirty-six at the time and supporting us—and my young mother, did the best they could.

Finally, spring term ended and my father arrived on the same train that had taken him away, hopped out, kissed my mother, and then looked at me, his child, his namesake, for the first time. In my baby book, a pink, dog-eared relic called "The Log of Life," my mother wrote that I had a wide grin, blue eyes, and black hair, just like my father.

My mother wondered and hoped—would it be love at first sight?

His first words were, "She looks like a papoose."

My father promptly got my mother pregnant again. He dropped out of school and moved from his college dorm into my grandmother's house.

Now we were a family. Three generations under one roof. A pedophile, a grandmother with unfortunate taste in men and a tendency to walk around naked, a pregnant teen mother, a college drop out, and me.

When my grandmother was at work and Homer was out of the house my parents would play a game with me that, until the end of their lives, brought them immense pleasure to recall—which they did often.

They'd scoop me up out of my crib, stand me on the ground in front of them, and then drop ice cubes down the back of my diaper. Watching me hop and howl around the house was better than watching the *Honeymooners* on television. They thought I was the funniest thing in town. They'd laugh themselves silly until the ice melted then rub Vaseline on my bottom and legs, hoping that my grandmother wouldn't find the welts. When the marks on my bottom faded, they'd do it all over again. My diaper dance was their favorite pastime.

They were just kids, after all, who had made a mistake— namely me—so why not just enjoy it?

I choose to believe my parents plopped ice down my diapers to amuse, not abuse. And I am quite certain my taste for attention and applause was born and bred during these early rear-citals.

Don't get me wrong, while performing my tidy-didy ditty, I also believe that deep within the early electric pulses of my forming cerebellum I sensed this iced-up butt jig was a clear, inarguable sign that it would be a slippery slog through childhood. I must have realized, while stomping around the house to their howls and whoops, that it was certainly going to be up to me to use whatever fancy foot-work was necessary to shuffle off to anywhere else.

My mother's appendix burst during the third trimester of carrying her second child, my brother. The doctors tried to therapeutically abort him, but he nonetheless hung on with what might have cost him his total allotment of grit and determination. He almost died again during birth because his umbilical cord was wrapped so tightly around his throat. Once my parents did get him home, his stomach burst and he had to have an operation that would cover his entire abdomen with stitches. The doctors sealed off part of his stomach and this procedure made it impossible for him to throw up. He would, quite literally, have to keep everything inside and down for his entire life.

My brother grew up skinny and small—and with an innate anger streak. Without fail, if I had a toy he would grab it and throw it in the trash, under the house, or out a window. It didn't matter how many reprimands or spankings he received—and he received many—he continued to toss and trash every chance he had. My mother could never let him play outside as a toddler because he would just start walking away. No matter the weather, no matter what games were being played or what treats had been laid out, or how busy the street traffic, he would go out the front door of wherever we were living and start walking away. He wasn't walking toward anything, just away.

My mother got pregnant again right after nearly dying giving birth to my brother. Once my sister was born my grandmother offered to treat my father and a friend to a vasectomy. Because vasectomies were illegal, bringing in two people garnered a discount and made it worth the quack's time to set up the surgery. My father actually found a pal to go with him, someone who did not have kids but had seen the three of us, I imagine.

After my father had been "fixed," my grandmother said it was time for him to stand on his own two feet and provide for his family. In other words, she had him spayed and then kicked the five of us out on our own.

To say my parents were in over their good-looking, movie-star wanna-be heads would be an understatement. They had basic formal education, but no skills. They had three babies, no jobs, and no prospects.

We left my grandmother's house, and were constantly on the move ... or run ...

Our first family apartment was above a hardware store where the rodents were so plentiful that my mother caught them in our cribs or in our bathtub and threw them in boiling water to kill them. Rather than becoming the actress or ballerina she dreamt of becoming, she sat home all day in a dank rat hole with crying babies. She busied herself cooking noodle and butter casseroles only to have my father throw them on the dingy linoleum floor in a tantrum, ashamed and angry that he couldn't afford to buy his family meat. They were twenty-one years old.

My father's first job was as a repo man—he was hired to take nice things away from people who had hoped they might keep them. It is no exaggeration to say he behaved as if this was also his job as a parent. When he got home from work, he liked to drink scotch and shoot at the pigeons that flocked around the dirt-square that was our backyard. If he killed enough of them, we ate those birds for dinner.

My mother spelled her name Patt, a short version of Patty Ann, so my father started spelling his name Ronn. I think they thought that by adding another letter to their names they would become worldly or exciting, like Olde Tavern or Le Sex Shoppe. But a rose, by any other name, is still a thorny person heading for disaster.

What I remember most from my earliest days is how much my mother adored my father. Every afternoon, before he got home from work, my mother would change her clothes and put on lipstick so that she would look her best when she greeted him. As far as she was concerned, he was the most brilliant, talented, and beautiful person in the world. In fact, his star burned so brightly in her eyes that she was blinded to anyone else around her—including her children.

As soon as my father got home, we kids were relegated to our rooms, where we'd watch TV shows while my parents ate dinner alone. It must have been while watching *I Love Lucy* or *Leave It to Beaver* that it occurred to each of us, in our own ways, that our parents were more situation than comedy.

I remember my father telling us a funny story about when he was young guy. "Was I around then, Daddy?" I asked innocently enough. "You've always been around!" he snapped. The lash of his resentment stung as much as his words had, but it was the truth, and you know, what they say about the truth is true—it hurts.

My father didn't allow my mother to drive until she was thirty, so if we had to go somewhere, we walked. Which means we didn't go anywhere. He didn't want her to take any classes without him, so she took none. He wouldn't allow her to join any clubs, or have any interests that didn't include him. I do know that she owned *How To Strip for Your Husband* and *How To Belly Dance for Your Husband* records because one time I found them while hunting through our stack of LP's for my *Little Toot* album.

At least she had hobbies.

She was once asked by a neighbor, who owned an advertising company, to pose with us three kids at a park for a local magazine ad. My father was at work so another man was hired to be "the father" in the scene. It turned out to be a beautiful serene shot with all of us looking happy while we fed the ducks. As payment we were given the original portrait. The neighbor told my mother to use the picture to get other advertising jobs because she was pretty enough to be a model and make some extra money. My father, upon seeing the photograph of his beautiful wife standing next to a "model" dad took a pen knife and carefully removed the face of the great pretender from the picture.

He ruined the photo and made me more than a little nervous regarding his mental stability. I was, I realize now, frankly surprised that he didn't hack us kids from the portrait as well.

If there had been a sampler cross-stitched with "Children Should Not Be Seen and Not Be Heard" it would have hung in our house with a spotlight on it like a fine painting. My mother collected "Hear No Evil, See No Evil, Speak No Evil" monkey statues, because, as she told visitors, "They remind me of the kids." It's true we were quiet. I think my parent's mistook this to be good behavior on our part and adherence to the "speak only when spoken to" school of child rearing. We were actually following another dictum, "If you don't have anything nice to say, don't say anything at all."

Since my father was no longer a big man on any campus, he decided to make us charter members of his new fan club. Membership was mandatory and it carried some privileges—it insured us food, clothing, and shelter. The annual dues, however, were pretty steep and continued to rise as the years accumulated.

My brother had very few friends growing up. In all of our years in the same house, I never saw anyone come over to ask if he could come out and play. He finally worked up the nerve to ask Charlie, a Native American boy from school, to come over for a swim one day. My sister and I were delighted to see him laughing and splashing with his friend like a normal boy. After their fun in the pool was over and Charlie left, my father asked my brother, "Is that kid an Indian?"

When my brother nodded yes, my father continued, "I thought so, now I will have to drain the pool."

He meant it.

I will never forget the warm, dry winds blowing through the western themed patio party my mother threw for one of my brother's early birthdays ... and I remember it mostly because no one came. Not one kid who was invited showed up. My sister and I swilled the root beer, ate the cake, played the games, and tried to be the party.

My brother never had another one.

I recall asking my father why he had been an only child. Without a pause he said, "When your parents reach perfection they stop. Take you, for example, we had to try two more times."

My sister, the "third times a charm" child, was fragile, quiet, and protected like the runt of the litter. She had my father's beautiful blue eyes—and a calm countenance that belied nerves that compelled her to rub her cuticles until they bled and agitated her skin into a perpetual rash. My sister still walks like someone who is afraid she may hurt herself. Because of these physical or emotional imperfections, or perhaps because they were running on parental fumes, she was treated with a benign neglect that, in comparison to the raising of my brother and I, appeared to be munificent.

Although we shared a room for most of our lives, we were more like cell mates than confidantes. We never physically marked the days of captivity on our walls, but I was counting them off in my head.

Once during naptime I played some circus music on the record player in our room, then I put on some white gloves and held a plastic pearl between my thumb and forefinger for her inspection. She watched, wide-eyed, as I "put" the pearl in my right ear, did a little twirl, and *Voilà!* I pulled the pearl (I had previously placed there) from my left ear. I had learned this trick watching Doug Henning on the *Mike Douglas Show*. Like so much of my heritage, the trick was only, as Henning would say, an "illusion." As the calliope music played on, I gave my sister a pearl and challenged her to try the trick. I stood by, quietly and supportively, as she shoved and shoved the tiny pearl deep into her ear canal. When it finally was in so deep that I couldn't see it, I walked over, pulled the needle up from the LP and told her, as my head shook in mock disappointment, that she just wasn't blessed with the gift of magic, like me.

She got ice cream on her way home from the emergency room. I got spanked.

To this day, I still owe her 1,000 back scratches.

One night I wheeled, dealed, and promised to return the favor—if she would scratch my back a thousand times. I lay on my stomach, on my twin bed, lost in bliss and on the one-thousandth lovely scratch, I pretended to be asleep. She shook me, slapped me, rolled me over, but I remained "sound asleep." My sister complained for weeks, months, and finally years about this shoddy treatment, but I never re-paid the debt.

I am not proud of this.

We still do not have a "got your back" relationship or anything even remotely close and I have only myself to blame. After all those years of drawing lines down the middle of the room, zipping up each other's dresses, listening to transistor radios under the covers, and dancing to the music of The Beatles, she is the one person in this world that I should know best, but I don't. In fact, I feel as though I hardly know her at all. We were kept too off-balance at home to get to know one another and I just didn't have the fortitude or foresight to move both of us out and up.

Like baby birds who huddle in the nest stretching and

cawing for a worm, seed, or a fluff of whatever the parent brings back to the nest, my brother, sister, and I became adroit in our attempts to win what affection and approval there was to be had from our mother. We subconsciously plotted desperate measures for recognition of our worth from our father. It was within this simmering cauldron of unmet yearning and unfulfilled acknowledgement that I found myself in direct competition with my siblings for the few scraps of requited love my parents could spare.

One way to narrow the competition, of course, is elimination. And all three of us, in our own warped and internal ways, employed this strategy however and whenever we could.

One day, while eating lunch in the backyard with the family, I saw my brother pick up a huge rock and start wobbling my way. I continued eating my hot dog and he continued on his staggering path closer and closer to where I was sitting by our mother. I turned to ask her what she thought he might be up to, and before I turned back, he had hoisted that ten pound rock into the air and let it drop—with a thud—on my head.

I recall bright yellow mustard squirting out onto the pavement, red blood dripping down my nose, and what seemed like the instantaneous appearance of a dish towel full of ice cubes being shoved against my forehead.

My parents simultaneously spanked my brother while discussing the possible hazards of watching too much Wile E. Coyote on Saturday mornings.

But I knew better. My brother wasn't inspired by cartoons; he was driven by the sheer will—the overwhelming need—for more than a speck of attention, even if it meant disposing of me.

From then on, I knew I needed to be on guard. Anything, a rock, a shoe, even a Christmas present, could become a weapon in a house that was electrified by limitless, but invisible currents of misplaced anger.

My brother's favorite holiday gift that same year was a plastic, grizzly bear hunting game called "Bop A Bear." When he opened it his eyes lit up like kerosene. The battery operated bear moved randomly around the room as my brother aimed a plastic rifle and bopped the thing with toy bullets. What in the world, I remember wondering, was St. Nick thinking giving a kid—who sacrifices dolls and uses a magnifying glass to torch houseflies—this shoot-to-kill game? As soon as he opened it I knew it would be "Bop a Sister" and, as expected, spent the remainder of that holiday dodging and then removing plastic bullets from my backside.

My sister, finding no ally in me, was always aligned with my brother. Having to share a room with me had resulted in her sleeping with earmuffs on and one eye open. So it was only fair that she, too, was often primed to take revenge on me or invent some form of sweet retaliation.

I don't recall the three us ever sharing one childhood moment that wasn't underpinned by the desire to win, place, or show. The competition to be the fair-haired child was so out of control, at one point after winning a third place ribbon at a swim meet, I stole a blue first place one to bring home. If I wasn't first—and shared with my parents the truth about being a third place finisher—it would have been Show and Hell.

We weren't victims of sibling rivalry, we were serfs at the mercy of royalty. Each child a mere court jester trying to stave off being banished or abandoned. The decree by which we all were governed was that no one in our family could be smarter, funnier, better looking, or more well-liked than my father.

How could we get someone like that—a father who would make you call him "My Lord" if he thought he could get away with it—to care about you, or even notice you? How, ultimately, could we win affection, appreciation, or approval from the soverign of our family?

This was the great existential question that dogged all three of us kids as we grew up. The only thing we had in common was being worn down from trying to jump into the orbit of my father's self-centered universe. We may as well have tried to defy gravity.

If we tired of the name-calling—or on rare occasion tried to stand up for ourselves, or fight a nasty remark from him—he would simply say, "Get over it." And so we did. My sister became overly-solicitous, my brother overly-pernicious, and I overly-ambitious.

In short, we did the best we could to overcompensate for the syndrome that we each suffered from—Parental Attention Deficit Disorder.

Every time I earned a badge as a substitute for my father's approval, I hand stitched it on to my sash. They have held neatly in place for over forty years. But, if you look behind the sash you see multi-colored threads running wild. Some are thick, others are thin, and some threads are crossing from one badge to another and back again. There is no symmetry or design, just a muddle of color and texture, dropped stitches, and haphazard knots.

My Heritage is created from what I remember and know, embroidered with pieces I have forgotten and remnants I have given away. It is sewn by memory with the common threads that have bound us together, hemmed to what I needed and wished for, and seamed together to form the fabric of my family life and the stories that I weave. And like those earnestly, albeit ineptly, tailored childhood sashes, what passes for accomplishment and success on the surface is, underneath, a real mess created by people who simply didn't know what they were doing.

Seeing new places, meeting new people, and exploring your neighborhood ... are some of the grandest adventures you can have ...

GIRL SCOUT BADGE BOOK

On My Way

My five-year-old brother is wrapping a can of Campbell's Pork and Beans in a red kerchief. I big sisterly say, "What in the world do you think you are doing?"

"I'm leaving home. I'm going to go live in the desert," he replies, full of courage and conviction, his little crew-cutted head down studiously examining his knot work.

"OK," I shrug. "Have a nice time and send me a postcard. Ha-ha." I joke as I stand outside his room watching him complete his pack job.

He finishes wrapping the canned beans. He adds a Bit-O-Honey candy bar and his plastic kazoo, for good measure, and throws the whole kit and kaboodle into the kerchief, then runs a stick through the bundle like the hobos do in the movies. I follow him as he trudges toward the living room and stops to address my parents, who are enjoying cocktail hour, before his dramatic exit through the front door.

"I am leaving," he begins, "and I won't be back," he finishes, jaw jutted out and clenched.

I am admiring his bravado.

"What's in the sack?" my father asks him.

"Beans."

"Are those your beans?"

"Uh ..."

"I believe you have my beans in your sack, give them back to me before you go."

My brother stares at my father. I have no idea what he is thinking, but I am afraid whatever it is he will say it.

Instead, he drops his handmade knapsack on the ground, straightens himself up, and strides out the door empty handed but full of intention.

My parents laugh, clink their glasses in a jolly cheer and then stand up, walk to the window, and watch my brother amble down our street.

"Aren't you going to stop him?" I ask, feeling like throwing up. Or maybe I'm just worried, it's hard for me to tell the difference.

"He's not going anywhere," my father smiles.

As if on cue, we see my brother make it to the end of the block, look both ways and turn back toward our house.

My father rushes to lock the front door before resuming his place on the couch next to my mother and they continue their happy hour, as if nothing has happened. My dejected little brother makes it up the driveway—walking like a movie criminal on his way to be hanged—approaches the front door, and turns the doorknob back and forth.

"I'll get it," I make a quick step in the right direction, but I am halted.

"Don't open the door Ronda," my father says.

There is no knocking. The doorknob remains still, for what seems to me like forever, before my brother gives in and knocks, faintly.

My father preens to the door, leans close to it and sing-song says, "Who is it?"

My brother doesn't answer. I think maybe I should scream his name in case my father has forgotten it.

"I said, who is it?" my father repeats and my mother walks across the room and joins him in a perverse version of "Knock, Knock Who's There?"

At last my brother gives in and says his name.

My parents open the door and look down on my brother— who looks right up at them and without missing a beat says,

"Which way is the desert?"

In our own ways and for our own reasons, it seemed like everyone in my family was trying to run away. And my brother wasn't the only one who lacked direction.

Through our multiple moves, the pendulum of houses and neighborhoods we lived in, and the temporary friendships I cultivated, school became my shelter and the teachers became reliable and reasonable signposts to point me On My Way.

Teachers liked me for the simple reason that I came to school way ahead of my peers. My parents had unwittingly created a highly effective and compulsory home schooling program that advanced my skills beyond my years. They believed that a child, most especially their child, did not need pre-school, or kindergarten, but would learn far more from a curriculum centered on fulfilling everyday tasks from the warmth of home.

For example, my earliest writing was a composition I penned to the store clerk at Manny's Food Mart stating that I was to buy a pack of cigarettes, "no filtured puleese," for my mother. My mother signed these notes, pointed the way to the store, and told me how much change I should get back.

Think of it—geography, math, and physical fitness in one fell swoop.

During our dinners, my father requested—OK, demanded—there be no "small talk" and for big talk we were asked—OK, required—to bring a new fact to be presented for his approval—OK, judgment.

Daily we kids would sift through newspapers, listen to the radio, or pull out the Encyclopedia Britannicas madly searching for an unusual story, factoid, or new word that would insure we garner "Best of Show." This meant you did not have to do the dinner dishes that night. The competition was fierce and once in awhile even my mother would get in on the mandatory "fun."

"Did you know that hummingbirds have no feet?" she contributed one night.

That was a humdinger! We all sat stunned, thinking about this statement and picturing the pitiable, perch-less, and diminutive bird who, according to her, was perpetually in flight.

"That's why you never see them land on anything," she continued not leaving well enough alone.

My father laughed, which meant we could all laugh, and addressing her as if she were a child—one he actually liked—he corrected her kind-heartedly.

She did have to do the dishes, though!

My brother—who once had to do the dinner dishes for a month because he claimed the J initial of his middle name "stands for Genius"— added insult to injury by bringing to the table the amazing fact that someone named "Duffy" had been President of the United States for thirty minutes.

"Really?" my father sounded intrigued. "When did this happen?"

"When another president died," my brother proudly proffered.

"Which president?"

"I don't know."

"Where did you find this story, a comic book?"

"No, sir, the encyclopedia."

"Well, I would like to see it."

My father excused my brother from the table and within moments he was back, triumphant, with the excerpt from the Britannica open and ready for inspection.

"Uh-huh, uh-huh," my father read, "yes, yes, it is true, there was a President Duffy for thirty minutes." And he gracefully closed the book and set it to the left of his dinner plate.

I couldn't believe it, my brother, who hardly ever won at anything, had actually pulled off an impressive victory. I couldn't even be envious because he was so jubilant. He was rightfully ecstatic and couldn't help but do a celebration bounce at his seat when my father, surely about to name him the winner of the week said ...

"Yes, President Duffy, for a full thirty minutes was president of ... the University of California."

Uh-oh.

"Not the United States, J for Genius, but president of a college. I suggest you do a more thorough reading job next time around. That will be a week of KP duty for you, Pinhead."

Thanks to the tutoring I received from dealing with shop clerks, competing with my mother and siblings during the dinner hour, and trying to please my father, I was prepared, when the time finally came, for entering a number of schools in a number of neighborhoods. I would go to four different schools in the first grade alone.

I liked everything about school—especially the part about being away from home for most of the day.

Anticipating the first day of school kept me awake all night deciding what clothes to wear, figuring out how to decorate the cigar box that would hold my pencils, looking forward to inhaling the smell of mimeographed handouts, or ingesting the art paste. Writing my name on the "This book Belongs to" and participating in the reading aloud from *Dick and Jane* books, "See Jane run, run Jane run," everything about school provided me a level of comfort and consolation I didn't even realize I was missing.

I did have one challenge about being in school all day and away from home. I was a site-specific thumb-sucker. I only sucked at home.

Anyway, I'd suck my thumb and rest my fingers on my nose while dragging my baby blanket behind me everywhere I went, but only within the confines of my house. I had done this from the time I was a toddler. My Binky was blue, with tiny red flowers scattered randomly, punctuated by little yellow stars that seemed to dash behind the billowing clouds of the pattern ... or at least it was once, but after a half-decade of washing and dragging it looked like it was only blue.

I annoyed my parents by begging them to let me bring my blanket to school on my first day, I was scared and thought it would be good to have a "lifelong friend" come with me. They, or more truthfully, my father, kiboshed that idea and sent me on my way unarmed.

Oh! How I missed my Binky that first long day at school. I had a difficult time concentrating and at one point I used my sweater as cold comfort, bunching it up in my lap and hanging it on my shoulder so I could nuzzle as necessary.

The moment I get home I race to my room, grab the pillow on my bed and toss it aside, knowing I will find Binky where I left it. My thumb is already in my mouth, warming up.

But, Binky is not there. My mouth dries up and my eyes began to water, *Where is my Binky?* I cry.

I began darting from room to room, closet to closet, in search of my Binky. I ask my mother if she knows where it is. She looks at me blankly. Next, I offer my younger brother and sister toy trade incentives to help me in my search. No luck.

By the time my father gets home, I am a wreck. I practically tackle him when he walks in the door, "Have you seen my Binky?" I shriek. "I can't find it anywhere, do you know where my blanket is?"

My father harshly answers that I am a "big girl now, not a baby," so I didn't need a baby blanket. He tells me that the "ratty, slobber-soaked thing" is in the garbage can and that's where it will stay. What I need is not some baby blanket, he lectures, "You need to grow up and be a first grader."

This blanket denial of something that I cherish and have formed a bond with has a profound effect on my attachment to and warmth for my father. I can't verbalize it, but I can feel it. I am betrayed, vulnerable and powerless ... and I don't like it.

It never occurs to me to go to the garbage and reclaim my beloved Binky. But I do wish I could whirling dervish past my father, like the cartoon Tasmanian Devil, wrapped in my beloved blanket, and leave him discombobulated and surrounded by destruction.

I turn to school for validation, for safety, and security. Because I am searching for so many things in one place I become a rabid over-achiever and within a month of starting first grade, I am told that I am going to be bumped up to second. This is the ultimate go-getter's school status symbol, skipping a grade!

Hold on. Not so fast.

I am in love.

My first, first grade teacher, Mrs. Pierce is the object of my deep affection. She is as round as she is high, and I disappear into her chest when she hugs me good morning, every morning. Her perfume smells of Fig Newtons and Pine Sol. Her approval and reciprocal love are all that I am aiming for, not some stinking promotion. Plus, I wonder, how can she let me go when I have worked so hard to please her? I want to believe she can never part with me, either.

Nope, losing Mrs. Pierce will be like having my blanket taken away all over again. I cannot—will not—let this second grade skip happen.

Like a prisoner about to be handed over to the guards, I sit hunched in a chair on the periphery of the room as Mrs. Pierce and my intended, second grade teacher explain the basis for the promotion to my parents and say they think this move is healthy for someone "bright and capable like Ronda."

My father sniggers and suggests school can't be that tough if I am going to skip a grade. My mother chalks up my doing well not to brains but to the fact that I have been a peoplepleaser my entire life (six years!) and have maybe good-willed them into thinking I am smart.

Sitting there listening to my parents, I allow myself a glistening daydream of full-time boarding school, or being kidnapped by gypsies. My dreams are doomed, of course. All I get is being sent to second grade with Mrs. Kellogg.

Her full name is The Dreaded Mrs. Kellogg. She has brassy, overly-bleached hair, permanently waved into a single, tight, small flip just below her ears. She is festooned with smudgy, charcoal drawn eyebrows that extended too far past her eyes, and bright red lipstick that is usually smeared beyond the corners of her mouth. She bears an unnerving resemblance to Bette Davis in *Whatever Happened to Baby Jane?*

And she smells like sour milk.

Mrs. Kellogg has a reputation for being mean enough to make even sixth grade boys cry and is so ornery that the gruff, whistle blowing, overweight, physical education teacher, Mr. Root, calls her "ma'am" and moves out of her way when they pass each other at school.

I am in a pickle. On the one hand, if I don't succeed, my father laughing at the whole idea of me being smart enough to skip a grade becomes valid. But if I make the switch I will be parking my bottom in a seat at The Dreaded's for the rest of the year. The choice is akin to the liver and lima beans dinner served weekly by my mother. No matter what I take a bite out of, I'll have a bad taste in my mouth and a stomach full of something I don't want.

The stress of it all is enough to make me a nervous wreck. And it does. The night before my second grade debut I lie in bed scratching, itching, thinking, scratching, tossing, turning, with some more thinking, followed by more scratching, until I can't take it anymore and get out of bed itching to get some help.

I wander out to the living room, stand in front of the television, face my parents, and announce,

"There is something wrong with me."

"I'll say," my father laughs, looking over at my mother, who chuckles at his hilarious comment.

Much to my horror, it is he, not my mother, who stands up and escorts me to the bathroom. He has me strip off my baby doll pajamas and step up onto the lid of the toilet to examine me. Being naked as a blue jay on a pedestal in front of my father is humiliating enough, but there is more to come. While examining me closely, pulling at the red marks, running his fingers over the most swollen and angry sores, he tells me I have hives, "something people get when there is something wrong in their head."

"Really, Mrs. Kellogg is the one who should be breaking out all over," he continues his pep talk as he has me step down and back into my PJ's.

He keeps going, saying she is going to be plenty sorry to have me in her class. I will probably need so much extra attention, he says, it will make her job tougher and teachers don't like hard work, that's why they become teachers. He says my hives will go away but that Mrs. Kellogg will break out in some nasty hives of her own when I walk into her classroom.

Listening to him gives my hives the hives.

He swabs each outbreak with a cotton ball dripping of cold, pale, pink Calamine lotion, wraps me in ace bandages, and sends me to bed with instructions not to scratch. I am like a corpse, not moving a muscle all night, barely breathing, caked in dried out, muddish anti-scratch glop. My mind, however, is ricocheting from plan to plan as I consider my alternatives to being sent to second grade the next day.

I rise early in the morning, drag myself to look into the bathroom mirror, and see that I am covered in chalky residue, the flesh colored bandages loose and dangling. I look like Boris Karloff in *The Mummy*. I am thankful, though, for my father's bedside manner because it is his doctoring-me-up pep talk that inspires my idea about how to retreat from my advancement.

Throughout my first day in second grade I barrage Mrs. Kellogg with constant questions and requests for extra help and direction. My father is right—it really annoys her. All during the remaining week in her classroom I whimper, I whine, I get up and roam around aimlessly, ask to go to the bathroom every half hour, hang like a baby vulture over her desk, and stare like the village idiot at the other students, complete with a bit of spittle dripping from my open mouth. In general, I make myself more of a nuisance than usual.

I am saving the best, or my worst, for our Friday spelling test. Mrs. Kellogg worked with me all week to spell crocodile, as that will be the toughest word on the verbal spelling test. "Spell it right," she whispers to me, a whiff of her sweetened and condensed milk breath turning my stomach, and I will "earn the respect and regard of the class and claim your right to be a second grader. If you blow it, you will have to go back to first grade," she threatens, thus falling perfectly into the palm of my little, first grade hand.

As soon as it is my turn to spell the thorny word, I stand with poise and assuredness, glance vacantly at my fellow and temporary classmates, and give what I know will be my second grade swan song. I slowly and deliberately, not wanting anyone to miss it but me, spelled "Croc-o-d-i-a-l."

Mrs. Kellogg grabs me by my elbow and escorts me briskly back to the first grade room. My feet barely touch the sidewalk as she shoves me into Mrs. Pierce's waiting bosom and fierce hug. The explanation for my return is, "socially immature," which is not the same, I reckon, as being dumb. I smile, burying myself in the living blanket that is Mrs.

Pierce. I have outsmarted the adults, but I keep it to myself. If anyone finds out, I might skip grades all the way to high school.

My triumph is short lived. We relocate whenever rent is raised, is due, jobs change, jobs are lost, or the grass is greener, or the wind blows west, and it isn't long before I find myself in another classroom, in another state.

I am only in my new school a week before it is time for my first report card.

Report? To whom, about what? I really have no clue what a report card is. I also don't know my teacher, the other kids, or my way home yet. Nonetheless, I am given a brown colored envelope not much bigger than my hand and told to take it home to my parents and have them sign it after looking at my report. This doesn't sound like a good thing to me.

Doing as I am told, I present the report card to my mother after walking home with only minor wrong turns. I haven't even looked at the thing, being too preoccupied making sure I don't get lost.

"Mommy, I have a report card!" I exclaim as I jump up on the couch beside her. She is watching Jack LaLanne, like she does every afternoon, sipping ice tea, and eating a chunk of chocolate—something called "Ayds" that is supposed to "keep her figure girlish."

This always confuses me. Wouldn't actually doing the exercises with Jack work as good as eating whatever Ayds is?

I proceed, "Let's open it, it's like a card from my teacher to you, or something. You have to sign it."

"Pwut it umm stable, forsh Daddy. Hell shine it."

Ayds are very sticky and her mouth is full, but I get it. I put it on the table for my father to sign and go outside to explore my new neighborhood.

"Let me see you write," my father, home now and swishing a tall, cold drink with a little swizzle stick plopped in it, says as I come inside from my trolling for potential chums in my new neighborhood expedition. He lays a piece of paper on the kitchen table, next to a couple of pencils that are already there.

"Hey, I have a report card from my new school, did you see it?" I say, not ignoring his command, but certainly distracted by curiosity about the contents.

"Yes, I did. You failed handwriting. Sit down right here."

I failed handwriting? Failed handwriting? How did I fail handwriting? And in only a week? My thoughts and heartbeat are accelerating as I take my seat at the table.

"What kind of moron fails handwriting? It's like failing breathing," he comforts me.

I am practically hyperventilating as he hands me the pencil.

"Write your name."

I feel hives coming on again.

I begin ... R ... O ... laboriously, N ... with my tongue bit now between my teeth, D ...

"What in the hell are you doing?" my father says, emphatic and involved enough to put down his drink.

"I'm printing, I am printing my name like I learned in school."

"What are you doing with your hand, your hand, Ronda, what is going on with *that* hand?" his finger, dripping with condensation from his gin and tonic, pushes on my right hand.

I look down at the offending appendage. I am fisting the pencil. This contortion works for me, it feels comfortable and it holds the pencil firmly in place to make the straight lines necessary for block printing my letters. But, I am also curving my hand totally inward, my hand is knotted, awkward, twisty. The pencil is practically touching my inner wrist.

"I don't know, I guess this is just how I write, I have my own style," I offer in my defense.

"For God's sake, you are turning your whole wrist in like a gimp, like you're a gawd damn cripple, keep your wrist straight," he commands, "try again, but this time keep your wrist straight, don't bend it."

I begin again, and am thumped on the head with the knuckles from my father's drink hand.

"Ronda!" my father yells, "turn your wrist back, NOW!"

I am scared straight for an instant and then as I continue writing, my wrist curves inward again. It is like there's a magnet inside my chest exerting a powerful force that pulls the #2 lead toward it.

"Tell you what we are going to do, Ronda, we are going fix this bad habit of yours this week, and there will be no more complaints from your teacher. You will be the best hand-writer in first grade. How does that sound?"

I can be the best at something? But my father will be my coach? This is my introduction to the concept of "God giveth and God taketh away."

"Sure," I rally. After all, I do want to be the best at something.

For the remaining first week of school my father comes home from work, sits with me at the kitchen table, and makes me write out the alphabet, letter by painful letter. Each time my wrist turns in, he swats it with a ruler.

Years later when Catholic friends will tell me about nuns and their rulers, I will just smile, knowing my superior father out-nunned them all.

By Friday I am cured of the curve and my father takes all the credit for the penmanship awards I receive throughout elementary school. "Ve haf vays to make you vin," he jokes and winks, like we share a fond memory. To this day German accents make my right hand twitch.

So it is, at my third school during my first year in public education I begin to understand the concept of grades, reports, winning and losing; and that the consequences of not measuring up amount to disregard at the least and something as harsh as the ruler at the most.

My next report card, which I look at as soon as I get it, is a testimony to my efforts and contains nothing but A's. Except down in the far left hand corner. There, in a singular category from the "A" grades in reading and writing appears a huge *F* in something titled "S-E-X."

I am panic-stricken. How in the world have I flunked a subject that I don't even remember learning? What will I tell my father and what needs correcting—or worse, his tutoring—this time around?

I take the long way to my latest home that afternoon, glancing at flowers, dogs, and cats, envying nature in all its "you don't have to go to school" glory. I drag my feet past the lawns of other laughing and carefree kids who did not have F's on their report cards, and tardily plod into our house.

"Where have you been?" my mother asks. "I was worried about you."

I break down instantly, the burden and shame of my failure too great to hide.

"Let me see that," my mother responds, grabbing for the report card. She laughs out loud.

"It's not funny, an *F* is not funny, I am going to be in fatal-with-a-capital-*F* trouble." I shout, dreading where in the world the swatting will land for this Failure.

"Honey, you got an *F* in sex, that stands for Female, it means you are a girl. That's all, it's not a grade, it's a fact, with a capital *F*!"

What gets graded and what doesn't, what is worth an "A" and what is worth an *F*, the inconsistency of our home addresses, the varied expectations of my many teachers, the thin bonds of friendships I can form, and the growing feeling that, at six years old, I might be the most mature person in my family gives me fits and starts as I head On My Way.

Is the musical life for you?

GIRL SCOUT BADGE BOOK

Making Music

"If I knew how to play piano, I would tickle the ivories during dinner, I could give us a little background music," I pluck out one evening while dining.

My family looks up from their dinner plates, first stare at me and then, in unison, turn to see my father's response.

"Could you play 'Far, Far Away'?" he puts his knife down, the edge facing toward the center of the dish.

He, so consequently we, has perfect etiquette.

Emily Post had nothing on us. We knew all the rules and ridiculous regulations. "Never pass the salt without the pepper." "Like a little ship at sea, I sail my spoon away from me."

When we dined together as a family, dinners were formal, served at 7 p.m. sharp, with quiet and intelligent conversation expected, though not often received. But uppermost in my father's rearing of his children was that we be mannerly.

In fact, when out in public, strangers would come up to us on a consistent basis to tell my parents what mannerly children they had. At a Denney's restaurant a woman stood for a full five minutes at our table lauding how "well behaved, respectful, and quiet these children are." The whole time she stood there I thought of passing her my paper napkin with the message "*Help Us*" scrawled across it.

At one point, I was so frustrated with the formality, the silence, and the downright fear of doing something wrong at the table that I brusquely asked my father "Why do we have to learn all this stuff? Why can't we just be like everybody else and talk with our mouths full and squirt ketchup from the bottle?"

Another rule: No bottles, cartons, or pitchers on the table.

My father quietly, sternly, and directly said to me, "I want you to be comfortable eating with princes or paupers. Knowing and utilizing good manners assures that you fit in anywhere you will ever go."

"I don't want to fit in everywhere," I bleated, after I finished chewing. "Who cares, except you, whether I put my fork down between bites? Why put us through all this rigmarole every stinking night, why use all these manners when it's just us, for crying out loud," I argued defiantly while holding my fork in mid-air, a definite no-no.

My father replied, "Fork down, Ronda," and then gives me the comeuppance that would shut me up about this topic for the remainder of my years at his table. He stated, with complete sincerity, "You'll never be in better company than you are now."

Please, please don't let this be true, I thought as I placed my fork at the correct angle and on the right spot of my plate.

Anyway, knowing that my father enjoyed the finer things in life, or at least wanted to, I hit him with the idea that piano playing would add a certain classy ambiance to our nightly repast. Not to mention that music lessons in some form were necessary for me to earn my Making Music badge.

"I can play any song you request, Daddy, it would be a pleasure to entertain my family." I play the innocent, pretending I don't get the "Can you play 'Far, Far Away'?" joke he delivered.

"Do you see a piano anywhere?"

"No but ... sometimes people rent them."

"Do you know how to play a piano?"

"Well, see, that's the thing ... I would like to take piano lessons."

"Well, I would like to be Steve McQueen."

Can a discussion be called a discussion if the other party doesn't engage? I think, already knowing that in our so-called discussions I never get what I am asking for, but my father always tells me I get what I deserve.

I remain pesky. I have to keep hitting the same key for the sake of my badge.

"I just think it would make my life complete to play piano, to learn how to play," I offer.

"No, we can't afford that."

"But, Daddy, I have it all figured out. It costs thirty-five cents for each pack of Lucky Strikes and almost two dollars for a bottle of Green Stripe scotch. That's the five dollars a week I need to pay for my lessons. If you give up scotch and cigarettes, I could become a pianist. And you would be a lot healthier."

I have rehearsed this line of reasoning, I never argue with my father without being prepared for every possible way he can say "no" to my requests.

"That's an impressive argument, Ronda. I applaud your efforts," he says sincerely. "But, let's say I give up my cigarettes and scotch, things I take pleasure in, and get run over by a truck next week. What fun would I have had? Besides, if I give up both scotch and smoking I won't be a very happy daddy—no matter how well you play piano—so no. End of discussion."

I did not see that truck coming.

Clearly I'm not going to hit the right chord at home, so I decide to get my musical education at school.

As a boy, my father played trumpet. In fact, his Conn silver horn with the pearl topped valves is wasting away in its black case in our closet. I bring it with me to school one day, approach the band teacher and blow at him, "I want to play trumpet."

"The band policy," he blares back, "clearly states that no girl can play trumpet in the school band. It could be bad for you when you grow up."

"Why?" I whine. "It's the only instrument I can get my hands on. I can't afford a flute or a violin. I want to learn music. I want to play music. Please?"

Unbeknownst to me at the time, a well-meaning and high-profile doctor, like the Surgeon General or Dr. Benjamin Spock, or some other big-male-in-charge type man declared that girls would damage their ovaries playing a horned instrument. Evidently, girls are only good for giving birth to the brass section.

In what's becoming the melody of my life, I know once again it is incumbent upon me to toot my own horn.

The opportunity to do so presents itself later that same week. My third grade teacher, Mrs. Lauman, brings in her electronic keyboard for show-and-tell. Although it is just another in a long line of thinly veiled attempts to avoid teaching, I consider it musical kismet.

In Mrs. Lauman's class we never learn to multiply or divide, like the other third graders, but we do garner important experience in rock hunting, frosting cupcakes, and gluing macaroni onto Joy dish soap bottles to make vases—which demands spray painting expertise as well.

"Who has taken piano lessons and would like to play my keyboard for the class?" Mrs. Lauman asks.

Raise your hand, the voice inside me urges, how tough can it be? Look at Joan over there waving her chubby hand. And Marilynn, of course she plays piano, and probably thirty other instruments, the bragger. If they can play the piano, anyone can play the piano. Including you.

My hand shoots up. And waves. I stop just short of the humiliating pig grunt and snort noises some kids make to be sure the teacher sees them.

"Ronda," Mrs. Lauman shocks me, "please come up and share some of your musical expertise with the class."

I have found it to be true, during my three long years as a public school student, that being an eager beaver repels a certain type of teacher, troop leader, family member, and peer. I am like a walking can of Raid Roach Repellent for Mrs. Lauman, so I didn't have high hopes of being her choice.

Besides, it can only be guilt that makes her select me from the dozen or more students who also raise their hands.

Mrs. Lauman and I went way back. We had history. On the first day of school Mrs. Lauman had passed out PTA membership request forms instructing parents, who wished to join, to place money in the attached envelope and send it back to school with their son or daughter.

My mother gave me the sealed envelope the next morning. At school, I handed it in and then the next thing I know Mrs. Lauman says, loud enough for students in the class-room down the hall, let alone mine, to hear,

"Ronda, did you take the money out of the envelope your parents sent in for the PTA?"

I had not taken any money or meddled with the envelope, and was astounded—and not a little annoyed—by the question. "If I was going to steal the money, why would I bother to turn in the envelope?" I asked thinking this was a plausible reply given the accusation being bandied about in front of my classmates. Looking for approval and agreement from them, I knowingly nodded and smiled their way.

This infuriated her and she moved faster than I had ever seen a woman her age move. She came at me, a wild look in her beady brown eyes, pulled me out of my chair and dragged my desk to the back of the room yelling the whole while, "You took the money. It was you. I know it was."

It was like too many years of chalk dust up her nose and coming to rest over her brain had finally erased her sanity in that once instant—and I was bearing the brunt.

Walking home later that day I pictured the unfortunate scene over and over again in my head. I could see the veins sticking out of her neck, I could hear the dragging desk, and I could taste the bile of being wrongly accused. By the time I entered the house and told my mother what happened at school that day, I had worked myself into brunts of my own.

My mother admitted that she had forgotten to put the money in the envelope before she sealed it, she found the three dollars in the kitchen cupboard after I had already left for school.

"You forgot?" I drawled.

"Well yes, but it's no big deal, take the money tomorrow. I signed the form."

"You don't understand, she humiliated me in front of the class, she moved my desk to the back, THE BACK! I have never been in the back and I don't like it," I frothed.

At dinner, mother told my father what happened and he was incensed. At my teacher, thank goodness. There were lots of "She has no right," and "What kind of a teacher," and "Public flogging" type things being said and my father, huffing and puffing, excused himself from the table.

What I could not know at that moment, but would find out soon enough, was what my father did behind the closed doors of his room. He wrote a scathing letter calling Mrs. Lauman every name in the book, every private piece of female anatomy, every son of a something name, every filthy thing his twenty-five-year-old self could come up with and more. He wrote of her stupidity, her narrow mind, and even her spinster clothing. The coup-de-grace was calling her the poster child for those who can, do; those who can't, teach.

I, of course, did not know what the letter said and my father had intended it to stay that way. But, when I complained the next morning about having to face my friends and be in that classroom with a teacher who thinks I am a crook, plus makes me sit in the back of the room like a delinquent, my mother's rare spark of sympathy was ignited.

My mother said, "Wait here." She marched elegantly back to her bedroom, got the letter my father had written, re-wrote it word for word in her clear and flowery handwriting, sealed that in an envelope, handed it to me on my way out the door with a sweet smile, a kiss on the cheek and these parting words, "Give this to your teacher and she will leave you alone from now on, after she apologizes to you."

I confidently handed Mrs. Lauman the envelope and stood right by her desk as she opened it and unfolded the letter— I wanted to be up front for her public apology. As she began to read the missive from home, a werewolf type transformation began. Her hands began to shake and her ears turned bright red. I could almost see smoke coming out of her nose and she threw the letter down as if it was on fire.

Now the veins on her neck bulged with those right in the middle of her forehead, swollen and pulsing, and her breathing became shallow and rapid. I thought I saw hair popping out of her chin and on the back of her hands.

"Who wrote this awful document?" she screamed at me.

"Um, my mother did ... she copied it from something my father wrote last night when I told him what you did to me." I began to back away from her desk, so slightly, hoping to be at more than an arm's reach away if she decided to bite me then and there.

Once again, in front of my class she barked at me, "I have never been more insulted in my entire life. Your parents are ignorant and you are still a conniving little thief."

At that she sent me off to outer Siberia, where my desk was parked, telling me to keep quiet all day. She did not want to hear word one from me.

And, I did not want to be a third grade werewolf so I maintained silence and distance.

Whether it is the gut wrenching guilt, the passing of the months softening her heart, or that her medication is now working, she does pick me to play the keyboard and I cannot be more thrilled. All is forgiven, sweet Mrs. Lauman, I think as I grin, pass by her desk, and tap on it lightly. If this little truce works, I might get my desk moved back up front!

As I strut toward the keyboard to the bilging sound of dismay from Joan—whom I pat on the top of her head as I prance by—I consider for a moment how I am going to pull this off.

To buy some time I brush off the bench where I will sit to play, and it suddenly strikes me that I have had some semi-professional experience in making melodies.

My grandmother, for once fully clothed, has let me sit beside her and twiddle the plastic keys on her Wurlitzer organ a few times. My tinkering creates a little movement my father calls "Gawdawful Racket," as in "knock off that gawdawful racket" but that I've re-named "Dance of the Sugar Plum Fairy."

I will simply improvise a reprise, I think. Mrs. Lauman will be none the wiser and my classmates will surely be impressed and entertained. I might be discovered and my desk and me will be back in the spotlight!

I take my seat at the coveted electric keyboard, flash my "skunk eating cabbage" look, say a polite thank you to my teacher, and begin my musical fairy tale.

Like Liberace, I play with drama and flair, introducing the name of my composition as I tinkle-tinkle-tinkle. "This is 'Dance of the Sugar Plum Fairy,' I say, rocking my body forward and back, closing my eyes. I play with my right hand on the high sounding keys—tinkle-tinkle. I pummel on the low sounding keys with my left hand—bum, de-bum, de-bum. Then—tinkle-bum-de-bum-tinkle—tinkling and bumming together in a cacophony of pure energy and, I believe, undeniable talent.

"Stop!" yells Mrs. Lauman as she rushes to the keyboard and unplugs it. "What in the world are you doing?" Mrs. Lauman pitches in a higher than usual register.

"An original composition," I reply, winking at the class like the youngest Lennon Sister from the *Lawrence Welk Show*.

I am promptly escorted back to my seat in the back forty,

yet again, so Joan Bovary could play something called a minuet.

Making Music is turning out to be much harder than watching the Mitch Miller show, *Sing Along with Mitch*, leads me to believe. The bouncing ball I seem to be following doesn't give me the lyrics I need, it just keeps going out of bounds.

By Christmas I am desperate for some music in my life and ask for my own ukulele. Instead I get a Betsy Wetsy doll. I am supposed to give her a bottle of water, which will run right through her, and then I get to change her diapers.

Santa definitely missed the beat on this one.

When the New Year begins, I turn my attentions to the possibility of being a singer. I can carry my instrument with me! The solution to my making music has been, literally, under my nose this whole time. I am already in the chorus, so I believe I have the basic training necessary to succeed in my latest melodious pursuit.

I decide to try out for a solo in the annual spring musical revue. I sign up for an audition slot and at the appointed hour present myself to the music teacher, Mrs. Walden, who wobbles in, smiles at me, and tries to recognize me through her bloodshot eyes.

"Why, Ronda, I didn't know you could sing," she slurs.

"I'm in your chorus," I remind her.

"Yes, of course dear, but I mean, really sing, like, say Robin Ross."

Robin Ross. My archrival and musical nemesis. She of the "classically trained voice," or so she keeps telling everyone in homeroom. "I sing at weddings and funerals for money," she boasts.

Funerals? I kill myself thinking, *At least the audience is tone deaf.* I also want to know how dead people can pay her.

Jealousy is not pretty.

Robin Ross wins all the solo spots in every pageant, play, and production. She sings the national anthem at all local sporting events and, in general, is a pain in my adagio.

"I'm an interesting alto, you said so," I say to Mrs. Walden.

"I did?" she looks at me like this is the first time she has seen me, "well, how about you let me hear you sing alone then?" She sits down.

At that moment, as if on cue, Robin Ross walks in.

"Oh, Robin," Mrs. Walden gushes, "Ronda here wants to sing a solo in the play. She is about to sing a song for me now. Come sit down next to me and we'll give a listen."

Robin walks past me, fluffs up her skirt, and sits down. Then, looking directly at me and rolling her eyes, says out loud "What are you singing, Rhoda?" but sends me the non-verbal message ... Don't bother.

"Is your name Rhoda? I thought it was Ronda," Mrs. Walden chirps as her many chins jiggle, "what will you be singing, Rhoda?"

Mis-directed enthusiasm, and merit badge requirements provoke me to stick to what I have started and I reply, "I will be singing the popular tune 'All I Do Is Dream Of You.'"

"You mean the song by Dr. Kildare?" Robin asks, her eyes growing wide in what I seriously mistake as awe.

"Yep," I say, defiant and confident—but hoping for a fire drill interruption to save me.

"I don't believe I know this song," Mrs. Walden says, thus explaining why she will not be accompanying me on the piano.

"All I Do Is Dream Of You" is a Top 40 hit, constantly being played on the radio. Richard Chamberlain is tearing up the charts with this tune. How can a music teacher not know "All I Do Is Dream Of You" I wonder. What in the world does she do when she goes home? Crawl into a casket and have Robin Ross sing to her?

I saunter over to the closet of wooden cubbies, also known as our nuclear bomb hiding spot, and stand inside and out of view so I can make an entrance. I take a deep breath and begin snapping my fingers. *A five, six, seven, eight*, and ... then I bop my singing self into the center of the room.

"All I do is dream of you (twirl)
The whole night through
With the dawn
I still go on
And dream of you (point coyly at music teacher and
    stunned, looking like a frog about to be gigged,
    classmate)
You're every thought
You're everything
You're every song
I ever sing
Summer, Winter, Autumn
And Spring" (dip, smile, twirl).

Always a believer in the big finish, no matter what I am doing (my mother is very tired of the "Ta-da" issued nightly after washing dishes, or maybe it is the bow while brandishing the dish towel) I glide back to the cubbies, hold onto the doorway arch with my left hand, and as I hit the last note I throw my head back, and disappear with a showy wave from my right hand.

I stand there a moment, expecting to hear wild applause. But it is eerily silent in the music room. I peek around the corner and spy Mrs. Walden and Robin just sitting there looking in my direction. I run from the closet, come to a stop in front of them, take a Broadway curtsy, and ... bupkis. No movement, no cheers, and no applause.

This is not my first or last "staring" ovation.

Evidently a bomb has finally gone off in the cubbies and it has my name all over it.

The solo for the spring revue goes to—Robin Ross.

Mrs. Walden thanks me for my heartfelt and "unusual" performance and suggests I keep singing in the chorus.

Is it months later, a week? I am not sure. I amble into our living room for a chat with my father about singing lessons. Our decorating style is shabby before that was chic. We have cast-offs from both sets of grandparent's furniture, some Goodwill finds, and garage sale steals. The only new piece of furniture we have is my father's orange "easy chair." Which is a laughable term because I never find approaching him while he is sitting there—or anywhere for that matter—easy.

"Daddy, how about me learning to sing?" I say timidly.

"You are still on this kick?" he looks up from his paper.

"Yes! I think I can be good at singing, I think I can be a paid performer. Robin Ross gets money for singing at funerals." I am, as usual, thinking ahead and considering money back on his investment a sure fire approach to get my lessons.

"All of this nonsense will be the death of me, I'm sure," my father replies. "OK, you really want to be a singer?"

"Yes!" I bounce.

And this "Yes!" is how I end up auditioning for my own parents.

"I would like you to prepare two songs for tomorrow tonight. Mother and I will listen to you sing and then we will decide about lessons."

"Great! What time tomorrow?" I am thrilled and pleased the answer is not an automatic "no."

"We'll call for you around 7 p.m." And, with that, he snaps the newspaper open and we maintain eye contact as I back away, almost bowing.

Now, the thing is, when you are growing up, you have no idea what happens in other houses. If you think about it at all, you think your friends kinda have the same experiences as you, the same type of parents, same meatloaf, same shoes from Phil's "Man Alive, Two for $5," same letdowns, triumphs, and punishments. There's always a Robin Ross in your way but you plow ahead. So I take my father's request in stride, figuring everyone who wants singing lessons has to try out in front of their parents.

For the remainder of the evening, and late into the next afternoon, I work on my big number, "Sunny" by Bobby Hebb. My rendition is two minutes and forty-four seconds of Arizona suburban soul. My father is a rabid Lena Horne fan, so I make sure to incorporate some of the facial expressions, grimaces, toothsome smiles, and the arching of eyebrows that have helped make her famous. My parents are sure to be awed by my song stylings. In fact, I am banking on an encore of the first tune, so I spend most of my rehearsal time on "Sunny."

At the appointed time—what else, cocktail hour—I get "the call." My brother and sister, hoping it is dinnertime, walk toward my destiny with me. My father, still dressed in his suit, welcomes us into the living room and suggests that my siblings view the audition from the hallway. I proceed past them, every inch the star I am sure to be after tonight. For the occasion I have chosen a little yellow dress, befitting the "Sunny" theme, with matching yellow rubber flip-flops. I feel like a daffodil about to bloom. As I pass my brother, he says, "You look like a stick of butter."

Our blue and green couch, improbably imprinted with Mt. Fuji and little "Chinamen" carrying water buckets over their shoulders, has been moved away from its usual position, facing the backyard window, and is planted in the middle of the living room aimed toward the kitchen. I am invited by my father to stand in the kitchen where there is more light and "better acoustics."

I have never heard of "a koo sticks" but I am not above grabbing at any advantage being thrown my way. Standing on the kitchen floor also gives me firmer footing than the lumpy, avocado green carpeting. Things are off to a good start.

My mother is already seated, holding a clipboard in her lap. She does not smile as I take my place in front of them; instead she looks at me and then down at her clipboard and appears very serious as she writes on the attached paper.

My father, who is holding a legal pad, takes his seat next to her, removes a pen from his shirt pocket with his right hand, clicks it open, and scribbles to warm up the ink, while his left hand swills his scotch on the rocks. He takes a sip and says, "Ronda, what will your first song be?"

"I will be performing the popular song 'Sunny.'"

Both parents scribble something on their notes, both

brother and sister are giggling in the hallway.

"Please, begin."

I clear my throat, smile, and belt out the song:

"Sunny, yesterday my life was filled with rain.
Sunny, you smiled at me and really eased the pain..."

I am building up to the chorus, complete with sweeping and open arms, like Dinah Shore in the "See The U.S.A. In Your Chevrolet" commercials,

"You gave to me your all and all,
Now I feel ten feet tall,
Oh, Sunny one so true, I love you."

I take a deep breath, do my best Lena Horne face—which I know looks uncannily similar to the face of the guy on the movie the *Hunchback of Notre Dame*—and am preparing for the big finish when my father interrupts.

"Ronda, you can stop here."

"Huh?" I ask, confused.

"Stop here."

More scribbling of notes ensues, but I am too far away and too short to see the writing on the wall. While I stand waiting, my brother and sister began a slow, cautious skulk down the hall. Perhaps they are intimidated by my superior talent?

"Do you have something else?" my father quizzes.

"Something, ah, else?" I stammer.

"Yes, another number?"

I can't really tell how this is going. There is something about the tone of his voice, the way my mother keeps her eyes on the clipboard in front of her. The manner with which my siblings disappeared into the shadows. I can feel my ears getting hot, my stomach starting to rumble, but I can't tell if the feedback I am getting and the feeling I have is good, like sick from excitement, or bad, like being a loser.

"I have a Troggs' song," I say haltingly.

"Proceed." My father says as he makes a series of small circles in the air with his right hand.

I make it through the first three stanzas of "Love Is All Around."

> "I feel it in my fingers, I feel it in my toes.
> Love is all around me and so the feeling grows."

"OK, thank you, that's it."

That's it? I wonder as I stare at them. *What's, that's it?*

"Yes," my father repeats, "that's it. That's all we need. Mother and I will discuss your appearance tonight after dinner and tell you in the morning what we have decided."

At that he yells for my brother and sister to come help move the furniture back into place. My first and only roadies help me push the couch back in place, all the while avoiding eye contact. We share a quiet dinner and go straight to bed.

I am too stoked by the prospects of something big happening in my life to sleep. I play the try-out over and over in my head, wondering which part my parents liked best ... and hoping they had liked me. While there are some unnerving similarities between this audition and the one I did for my music teacher, these people are my flesh and blood, they are supposed to give me the part. I am, by birthright, their top pick.

I get up early the next morning, dress for school, gather my books, set the breakfast table, humming all the while, imagining telling all my friends—especially Robin Ross—the big news about my singing lessons.

Eventually everyone but my father is at the table for breakfast. I am eating my Alpha-Bits when he walks in, pulls out his chair, and sits down.

"Good morning," I say, sharing my best I-am-ready-for-good-news smile.

"Good morning."

"Well, Daddy, what do you think?" I rush.

"Ronda, your mother and I talked about this a long time. People who become famous singers have very distinctive voices. People like Lena Horne, Eartha Kitt, Frank Sinatra—you know who they are the minute you hear them sing."

My mind races ahead, I knew the Lena Horne bit would do the trick. My heart is beating out of my chest as I wait for the "yes" that will change the trajectory of my life.

"You don't have a voice like that," he shatters my reverie. "You have an ordinary voice. It's even somewhat pleasant. But you will never make it as a professional singer. So, no, Ronda. We don't think you should waste your time or our money on voice lessons."

I feel my ears flush hot again and my churning stomach now contains my sunken heart. I feel too heavy and deflated to argue. I want to spell out some nasty word in reply with the floating letters of my cereal.

Which is worse? I wonder as I try to digest his assessment. Being told no ... or being ordinary?

Some people are born average and others have it thrust upon them. I mull over the recent concert of events and I come to the conclusion that the only way not to be ordinary and win the Making Music badge is going to take an extreme move, something extraordinary and worthy of a "Bravo"..., and I know what that something is. I sign up for yet another audition, but this time at a place where no one related to me will be, the *Lew King Rangers Show.*

Cowboy-hatted, bolo tie wearing, boot stomping Lew King hosts a show that is the Phoenix version of the national *Ted Mack and the Original Amateur Hour.* Young hopefuls under the age of eighteen from all over Arizona descend upon Stage Three of the local CBS affiliate and try out for a spot to be a Lew King Ranger. One of the future Miss America's, Vonda Kaye Van Dyke, won first place on the show doing ventriloquism. Lew "discovered" an eighth grader named Wayne Newton. Isn't it possible that I'll be discovered, too? After all, I have audition experience, there is no tougher audience than my father, and I have so much determination that it has somehow escaped me that talent might also be a requisite.

Seeing and loving the movie version of the *Sound of Music* on a recent school field trip, I decide to sing a number from the show. To rehearse, I enlist my mother, along with my grandmother, the patron of many arts including strip tease and my mother's girlhood dance lessons. For an entire day we work on the song, "My Favorite Things."

Grandma, in a stroke of choreographic brilliance, suggests I shake my leg and then hit my arm and murmur a little "Ow" when I come to the line "When the dog bites, when the bee stings." This stuff is gold. I am ready, willing, and confident.

I beg my father to take me to the audition on the following Saturday, since my mother doesn't know how to drive. I am slated for a 3 p.m. audition and told to arrive at 1 p.m. so I don't interrupt other performers. "Performers." I love the sound of that and the idea that I might be one.

"1 p.m. on a Saturday? I'll miss my tennis game, can't you ride with a friend?" my father complains.

"None of my friends are doing this. Please! I have an audition!"

He reluctantly agrees to take me, making me promise that this will be the end of all this "stupid music stuff." He even says that he should get my music badge for all the time and trouble this is causing him. And he reminds me that my home version of an audition had not been so great, so I shouldn't get my hopes up.

As usual, he really knows how to put a song in my heart!

We walk onto the CBS lot together, my father and me, through a dark hallway that leads to a brightly lit sound stage, a piano, and an assortment of young, talented kids. Sitting down on the cold metal folding chairs that line the back wall we wait for my turn. For over two unfolding hours of personal torture I watch as trained, gifted, precociously talented children from around the state belt out arias, dance the *Nutcracker,* twirl fire batons, juggle bowling pins and, in general, make it clear I am quite a ways from extraordinary. And dangerously close to below average.

My father goes outside to have a smoke. When he comes back, the clock is edging perilously close to my audition time. I run up to him, frantic, tears forming,

"Please take me home, I can't do this. I don't belong here, please, let's go, please, I can't sing."

"We're not leaving until you do what you signed up for," says my father, sternly.

"Please, Daddy, I can't do this, I will make a fool of myself, I am begging you, begging you, take me home. You are right, I'm not a singer, I'll never ask again, but please don't make me sing in front of these people."

"No. You started this, you finish this."

"Ronda Beaman?" the casting person calls, "Ronda Beaman, your turn."

"I'm, I'm ..." my father puts his hands squarely on my shoulders and squeezes, "I'm not ready!" I shout.

The casting director takes one look at sorrowful me and says, "OK, let us know when you are," and calls the next entertainer up. I grow ever more miserable when a pint sized dynamo belts out opera, in Italian—while doing gymnastics. She's singing while in a backbend!

I may not sing or dance, I may not paint, I may not juggle or do impressions, I cannot even do a backbend, but I do have a strong sense of survival, and in this case, I know surviving means waiting until everyone else auditions and then choking through my song with no one else in the room. So, that is what I do. I wait it out, crying, sobbing, still hoping for pity, until finally, there is only my father, me, the piano player, and the casting director sitting together on Stage Three.

"Are you ready, Ronda?" the casting guy says kindly. I can tell by his face he feels bad for me. Heck, I feel bad for me. I walk slowly forward with the sheet music I bought—using my allowance money—from Merkle's Music Emporium in the mall. The piano man, tired from a day of auditions and ready to go home, says,

"What key, kid?"

What key? I think. *What key? Key to what?*

All I know is a door is closing and locking for me at this moment.

I weakly answer that I want the black key. The piano player acquiesces and hits one black key first and I blubber my way through "My Favorite Things" until I, at last, reach the crescendo, the final stanza ...

"And then I don't feel so bad."

I don't need to re-enact the dog bite or bee sting because I am already wailing like a stuck pig. It is painfully obvious I am out of my element and no amount of raindrops-on-roses or whiskers-on-kittens is going to help me at this point.

"Thank you, Ronda," the casting director circles my name in red as he says good-bye.

As if doing poorly isn't punishment enough, why do all adults make disgrace worse by using a red pencil? I think, while hanging my head and walking to our scalding car, burning the back of my legs as I crawl into the front seat. Why not calming blue, or just a plain black check mark or circle around my name? Why red? It's like a slap against my face, which is already red enough.

When I get home, my mother is there, waiting, with a cake she's made for me in the shape of a star with the message "For Our Little Star" scrawled across it in orange frosting. I take a big piece of cake but the truth is I am eating humble pie. I will not be a star or even a singer. I will never be a Lew King Ranger.

Oral reports, chorus outings, and a 100 percent on a city-wide test identifying composers at the Westward Ho Hotel, eventually win me my badge. The instrumental lesson I really learn, however, is that my life is my own composition. How I conduct myself in the highs and lows is way more important than if other people—like say my parents—say I fail or tell me I am ordinary.

But, geez, is it too much to ask for a smidge of encouragement? I bet Mouseketeer Annette and Wayne Newton failed auditions too, and they kept singing. OK, OK, sure they do have talent ... but I must be good at something. I just haven't found out what that something is ... yet. One of my favorite words—yet. Because it means I'm not finished. It's not over. I'm not done.

So, I decide to keep practicing being me until I'm good at it. That way, no matter what I do with my life, I will still be Making Music.

Dance Badge

I am sitting cross-legged on the sun-warmed concrete of the breezeway after school, playing jacks with Swanee Burkhart. The main reason I like her is her name. I have slips of paper at home, stuck within the pages of my diary, scribbled with all the names I might use when I became Ronda renowned. My first pick so far is "Ronda Rainier," inspired by an article about Princess Grace of Monaco that I read in *Life* magazine. But I am toying with Ronda Real, although it may sound too much like a comic book character. I am taking my time deciding—and getting famous apparently—but I figure I will know what I should be named when I hear it. So I keep collecting names.

I also love my friends Desi Van dePol, Bambi Hefner, and Genkie Stocks, who everyone calls Stinky Socks, for their name's sake. I would choose being called Stinky over being forgotten any day. If you say "Swanee" or "Genkie," everyone at school knows who you are talking about. I want a name like that, that almost defines your destiny. I mean, who else could someone named Vonda Kaye Van Dyke be except Miss America? The closest my name has gotten to memorable, so far, is a chant the boys lifted from a Honda motorcycle ad, "Nifty, Thrifty, Ronda Fifty." I don't really know what it means, but it has my name in it, they sing it on the playground, so I like it.

Then there is Clyde, another new girl at school who not only has a memorable name, she comes with a bonus, a give-away she uses to create interest in her. Like when a Libby glass tumbler is included in a box of detergent or a decoder ring is found in a box of Wheaties. Every day she brings Jello Chocolate Pudding mix, I mean just the dry mix, in a box, and eats from it all day long. She wets her finger, sticks it in the box, and "presto" her finger is a chocolate sucker. Plus she shares! By the time the Jello box is empty, at least thirty wet fingers from thirty different hands have partic-ipated. Everyone knows and likes Clyde the human pudding pop.

Yep, I need a better name or a gimmick. Ronny or even Rawn? How about combining first and middle names to become Andra Beaman, and giving pieces of Beeman's gum to everyone? Nah, it all lacks a naturalness that my friends' names possess. Maybe cinnamon sugar mixed in a bag would work ... and hey! Call myself Cinnamon!

This is the pressing issue I am mulling over as I dominate the jacks game I am playing with Swanee, who hasn't even had her turn yet.

I'm on my three-sies when I hear a loud rat-a-tat-tat rumbling our way. What the heck? I think, grabbing my official, good luck, golf ball in mid-air and looking toward the offending ruckus.

Barbara Cadkin is stomping our way in the most striking patent leather black shoes I have ever seen. They tie with red velvet ribbons. And with every step she takes, the tapping sound coming from her soles makes me want to get up and Fred Astaire right then and there. I would not want to trade names with Barbara, but those shoes, oh my gosh, those shoes. They are far better than pudding.

I fight back my drool, but cannot lick my envy.

Barbara's shoes out-do the now pathetic-in-comparison ruby slippers on Dorothy's feet when she danced her way to Oz. I am embarrassed being seen doing something as inane and simple as jacks, a kid's game. And being with Swanee who is truly an odd duck, so unsophisticated, so plain, so wearing tennis shoes. Like me.

Nonchalantly, although I am all chalant inside, I raise my gaze upward from my cement seat at the humble peasant's game and greet Barbara, trying so, so hard to make eye contact. I must not stare at her shoes. I will not give her the satisfaction. Plus I am not altogether certain that I won't go blind if I stare at them too long.

"Hey Barb," I toss my head up pertly and am surprised by the higher than normal pitch in my voice, "whatcha doing?"

"I have dance school today," she replies, not missing a step. She quickly clomps by, the clicking of her shoes reverberating through my nervous system and shaking my little tin jacks.

"Bragger," says Swanee.

With reason, I think gathering up my jacks, bored with childish games, putting them in the little burlap sack that had once held my Gold Rocks Nugget Bubble Gum. I say a grim good-bye to Swanee and walk, in my way too quiet

Keds, toward the Circle K market, all the while formulating my next badge attack.

Why didn't I think of this before? Voice lessons, piano or trumpet, or being in a band all relied on outside equipment that I didn't or couldn't have. But to dance, all I need is feet. Check.

With conviction that my feet are as good as Barbara's, I point both of them toward the Jerri Johnson School of Dance.

I have seen Jerri Johnson's school a million times, it's in between the Circle K where I buy cigarettes for mother, and a hair salon. Now I know it's also where I will find my fate.

The walk from school to the seedy strip mall is long enough for me to solidify my newest scheme to earn a badge or get discovered, whichever comes first.

I can't just be talented, I realize, I have to be talented *at* something. It might as well be dance.

I need money for dance lessons so—and it takes me no time to think of this—I first enter Circle K and ask the clerk if I can welcome customers and help them with their bags, all for twenty-five cents a day.

I think of being a greeter way before Sam Walton.

I explain to the uninterested employee behind the counter that I need to take one dancing lesson a week next door for Girl Scouts. It is my only way to earn the Dance Badge, and it will be so impressive—I continue, once I am famous—to let the newspapers know this is the store that launched my career.

The large man behind the counter, wearing what can only be described as a suspiciously stained white t-shirt and sporting a tattoo of a smiling gila monster crawling up his forearm, stares at me like I am something he might feed a pet snake he surely owns, and then finally suggests I just steal a candy bar like everyone else my age.

Undaunted, I proceed to the hair salon next door. It is resplendent in pink and reeks of the Toni home perms my mother gives me annually on Labor Day weekend. A woman up front with a brassy red beehive greets me with, "Are you Melva?"

"No, I'm Ronda." I smile the best I can while holding my breath.

"I thought you said Melva, but my phone don't work that good. Here, sit down, Melva."

"Huh? You mean Ronda?"

"Whatever, just sit down and I'll get your cut done."

"Oh no, I didn't come here for a cut."

"Then why did you make an appointment, Melva?"

"I didn't make an appointment, I'm Ronda."

"Well, where's Melva?"

Would not trade names with this one, either, I think and then say, "Look, I don't know where Melva is, I just came here to see if I can get a job sweeping hair up for you, for twenty-five cents a day."

Again, like I did at Circle K, I explain my goals and I'm generous in my promise to let the world know about her salon, once the world knows about me.

"You don't want no haircut?" the beehived woman said.

"No, I want to sweep."

"Do you see any hair on this floor?"

Just like home, I think, with adults asking questions that mean they think you are stupid and are mere detours before they get around to saying no.

"No, ma'am," I reply.

"Do you see Melva, or anyone else in one of my chairs getting a haircut so there will be hair on the floor?"

"No."

"Well, you just answered your own question about getting a job here."

Back out on the sidewalk, in the bright Phoenix sun, I draw in some non-Toni air, and consider my remaining dance fund opportunities.

Why not go straight to the source? Enough pussy-footing around. Ask Jerri Johnson herself. Go to the top, I coach myself.

I push open the door to the Jerri Johnson School of Dance and I'm greeted by the sound of tap shoes on a wood floor and see at least a dozen girls my age wearing colorful leotards and tutus. *Oh, what could be grander than to own my own tutu?* I sigh, watching in awe all the girls in the studio who are leaping and laughing to a Paul Revere & the Raiders song called "Kicks." There are wall-to-wall mirrors so the girls can watch themselves as they leap and jump. Miss Jerri

Johnson—yes, she has a trade-able name I think—is a small, elegant older woman of at least forty, who is tapping a stick to the beat and calling out moving directions to the girls.

"To the left, to the left, dainty, girls, dainty," she commands and they try to do what she says.

I feel plugged in, like an electric current is charging through me. It's like nothing I have ever felt in my entire decade of living.

I belong here, I most definitely belong here. I daydream in fast forward to my life from this day on and it includes my own skyscraper dance studio with my name over the door. Maybe I will change my name to Robbie or Shilo, and create programs to help other young and deserving girls dance ...

"May I help you?" Miss Johnson breaks into my dance trance and halts the lesson. She and the dozen or so girls look gracefully my way.

"Oh yes," I answer, "you can help me. I want dance lessons and I am willing to work for them."

Miss Jerri Johnson is a good audience as I tell my stories about attempting negotiation with my father to collect scotch and cigarette money, my hiring interview with the gila monster man at Circle K, all my dashed attempts to play music, get on Lew King, how my hair salon career was cut short, and my finale about how I have humbled myself, repeatedly, all in the name of belonging and badges.

"So, you see Miss Johnson, I am dedicated and determined. I will do anything, no job is too big or too small, I will come work everyday—in trade for one lesson a week."

Miss Jerri Johnson misses my pointe.

Following my pitch to keep the mirrors of her studio clean or buff the scuff marks off her wood floor in exchange for lessons she begins to understand that "willing to work for them" does not mean practice, but that I, literally, want to work for my dance lessons.

I have already established that good answers from adults never start with sarcastic questions. Now I learn that replies like "I am afraid ...," or "I am sorry but ...," or "I know you can appreciate ...," have nowhere good to go, either.

"No," she says to me. "I am afraid if I give you this opportunity, blah, de blah ... I am sorry but other girls in similar circumstances ... blah ... I know you can appreciate my position ... blah, blah, blah."

By now the dancing girls who have been watching and listening to our exchange are self-conscious for me. I don't have a come back for Miss Jerri Johnson's "no," and something inside me knows I never will come back.

You'll be sorry someday, Miss Jerri, who wants your name, who has ever heard of you anyhow, and if you are any kind of good, what are you doing stuck in this nothing studio in the desert? Huh, Johnson? I mumble as I slink out of the place.

I should have kept playing jacks with Swanee, I think as I wander home. I already know how to do jacks, I win at jacks, I am not humiliated when I play jacks. I should stick to stuff I know, stuff I am good at, that's all.

But, I argue with myself, tetherball and jacks are not exactly Olympic events. If I only do what I'm good at, well, so far it's looking like there's no big future in that.

By the time I am standing in front of my house, I take a page from the scouts and I make a pledge of my own. Because I love my badges, because I choose not to listen to "no" and continue to search for "yes," and because I am ten, I choose to move forward—that is I choose dance instead of done. And I swear that, when I grow up, I will help kids, not stand in their way, so help me, God.

I get the God part from watching the oath taken by witnesses who are called to testify on the *Perry Mason* show.

"What's that hissing noise?" my father asks at dinner. "Did someone let the air out of your tires, Ronda Ann?"

My mother must have told him about my failed expedition to the strip mall.

"I have to hand it you, you don't give up easily. Being gritty will serve you well in life. You won't know how to dance or sing, mind you, but you will be a dogged little person who works through all the 'no' that is bound to keep coming your way." He smiles and shakes his head from side-to-side.

If luck can be defined as preparation meeting opportunity, I will say that I am lucky. I am always prepared to take advantage of any opportunity.

Within the month following my non-debut at the dance school, my teacher announces one day, "We need tap dancers for the 'Frosty the Snowman' number in the upcoming Holiday Pageant. Please raise your hand if you have taken tap dancing lessons for at least two years."

As if a survival instinct, my brain fires on all cylinders and the wheels of fortune begin turning. Who needs two years of lessons, who needs lessons? I saw those girls at Jerri Johnson's, they were no great shakes.

Like Bobo, my plastic punching bag clown that is filled with sand to weigh down his feet, life keeps thumping my ambition and ideas, but I keep popping back up, landing on my feet ... and raising my hand.

In what must be a nod to self-esteem building, everyone who raises a hand gets picked for the dance line, except Jimmy Carson. "Boys cannot be snow fairies," my teacher tells him, so she lets Jimmy be the snowman.

Wait, now he's the star? This frosts me. How is it that if I want to play trumpet in the band I am told no and shoved out the door, but if a boy wants to do something and is told no, he gets to do something even better? I might do better in the world if I change my name to Ron, I huff.

I have been selected, and this is some comfort, so now I need to learn how to tap, get some shoes, and get dancing. I figure I can do all of this at lunch.

As a rule I prefer to bring peanut butter sandwiches from home in a red plaid lunch box with the words "Safety First is an Important Rule, At Home, At Play, and in Your School" proudly emblazoned across the front. It makes me a favorite with teachers and crossing guards alike, and you can never have too many friends in high places. And I enjoy my smushed peanut butter sandwich way more than the usual school fare of food like neon yellow macaroni and cheese with corn and peas mixed in called "Fiesta Pasta," or the salad made with raisins and shredded carrots they tried to pass off as "Golden Glow." Clearly, the person who decides what to call the dubious school lunch foods would be an ideal person to help me invent my more creative and interesting name.

But, as fate has it, this is chili con carne with cinnamon roll day at our cafeteria. C and C, as the lunch lexicon goes, is my favorite lunch, heck, meal, of all time. It appeals to everyone at school regardless of gender or grade. It is spicy, it is sugary, it is the perfect lunch for all of the children of pre-metropolitan Phoenix; namely Mexicans and WASPS with asthma.

The desire to buy this lunch can drive kids to do unseemly acts. Rufus King sells looks at his sister Carolyn who pulls up her blouse for twenty-five cents a peek to buy lunch on C and C days. He also showcases his sister to buy snow cones at baseball games, icees after school, and many days in between, but still ...

I have a deal to seal so I dump my lunch pail back in my homeroom and reach into my regulation Girl Scout wallet which contains my one dollar and seventy-five cents of allowance. I race back to the lunch line hoping to find the dance doyenne of our school, the same Barbara Cadkin of the coveted red-velvet-bowed tap shoes.

Dancer, fellow scout, and Jewish, Barbara Cadkin. Despite my desire to walk in her tap shoes and out earn her in badges, we are kinda friends. She once took me to temple on Sabbath and explained she and her family were "chosen." I asked her, "chosen for what?"

It is a mad dash up and down the not exactly straight-and-organized lunch line twice before I find her, holding a blue flowered lunch pail, waiting to purchase her half pint of milk.

"Barbara, I am so glad I found you, isn't it great we are both *chosen* for the Holiday Pageant dance number?" I figure it can't hurt to take advantage of our previous, shared religious connection.

"To celebrate," I add, "let me buy you lunch." My father once said that all Jewish people like it when you pay for lunch, or dinner, or pay always so they don't have to pay for anything. It is part of their heritage, he told me.

Barbara could not resist the lure of the chili and cinnamon roll, I felt confident.

"Sure!"

"Cool." I look up at Barbara, literally, as she is at least six inches taller than me, and wait in line for my bowl of chili. After the polite small talk about spelling words that week and tetherball tactics, I move, casually I believe, to the topic of the dance number for the show and delve right into my ulterior motive. I explain that my parents have hit a rough patch (I am sure they will be hitting something soon if they find out about this) and sold my beloved tap shoes.

"You know, the shoes I have used for the past two years? Yep, sold them to help out at home," I pinocchio.

"I didn't know you were taking dance class, where do you go?" Barbara asks.

"Um, go? Uh, I don't really 'go' anywhere, it's a, it's more, well, I take private lessons." I exhale with relief at coming up with this answer.

"Wow, that is expensive." Barbara is impressed.

I am in deep.

"We aren't suppose to talk about it, so don't tell. It's pretty tough ... and now I don't have shoes to use for the pageant." I look down at my lunch, afraid to make eye contact, and attempt to look sad.

"Then why are you buying lunch? Shouldn't you be saving your money?"

Man, that Barbara Cadkin ... a tough and sharp customer.

My mother told me that each time I lie, the whites of my

eyes turn green, and whomever I am lying to will see it. By now the whites of my eyes must have gone from pale green to lime green and I was surely on my way to deep, dark forest green.

"Well, the school, yeah, the school is helping me, they give me lunch money once a week to help. I didn't use it last week so I can share with you today."

"Oh, Ronda, you don't have to do this."

"No big deal, I do it for really good friends like you, Barbara." I almost cry, but from stooping so low, not for my supposed lost shoes and current poverty, like Barbara thinks.

"Do you have some taps I can borrow?" I gulp.

"Well, I just got new shoes. They are so sweet. They tie with red velvet bows."

"Oh, yeah, I saw you walking in them the other day. They are really something," I kiss up.

"I guess you can use mine from second grade," Barbara says, "if you give me your cinnamon roll."

Barbara Cadkin, first worried about sharing my charity with her and the next minute driving a hard bargain. I have already bought her lunch, now she is gonna glutton a second roll. But, I am in no position to argue that my chili will be no good without the cinnamon roll, knowing my tapping will be no good without the shoes.

"Deal," I say as I watch her scarf down my cinnamon roll.

It is a small price to pay, I comfort myself while envisioning her tap shoes on my soles.

After school I walk home with Barbara and pick up her second grade toss-off taps. Bidding her good-bye and heading to my house alone, clutching the shoes, I plunge deeper into the tangled web I am weaving. I have to plan my next steps carefully to create a plausible home version of why I have Barbara's shoes. Otherwise I know from experience I will have to take them back.

❧

My parents, turns out, did pay attention to me. It just isn't the kind of attention I wanted.

Not long ago, but long before the Circle K clerk suggested it, I did steal, but not a candy bar. I stole a pack of Juicy Fruit from a 7-Eleven. I don't know why. It was easy, it was only a nickel, heck, one pack of gum wouldn't even be missed. I guess I was experimenting with my dark side. Later that same day I had forgotten all about my life of crime and was chomping away on my illicit gains, playing cards with my sister, and my father walks in, watches us for a minute, and then says,

"Ronda, where did you get the gum?"

"Huh?"

"The gum, in your mouth, where did you get it?"

I kept my eyes on the hand I had just been dealt and say, "7-Eleven" which I feel confident saying because it is the truth. I did, in fact, get the gum from 7-Eleven.

"Ronda, put the cards down and look at me. Did you buy the gum?"

I wanted to spit the gum out and make a run for it. But I

persisted in creating an even stickier situation by answering "Yes, yes, I bought it at 7-Eleven."

"Where, might I ask, did you get the nickel?"

The Bible says that God keeps his eyes on the sparrow. Evidently my father had been keeping his eyes on me. He watched so closely that he knew I didn't even have five lousy pennies to rub together. Our father, who was not in heaven, knew I could not have bought the gum without taking a nickel or stealing the gum.

Following my tearful admission that yes, I had robbed the store, I was promptly taken back to 7-Eleven, walked up to the counter by my father while holding the half-used pack of gum in my offending mitt, and told to give my confession at the altar of the cash register.

I apologized for my sin and said I truly was sorry.

Throw in mortified.

I pushed the open pack of gum across the counter toward the day-shift clerk, turned to leave the store and sighed in relief—lesson learned.

But, oh no.

I think my father must have called ahead and told the acolyte working the cash register he was bringing in the perpetrator in the name of justice and the American way, because this guy called me back and proceeded to preach about ill gotten gains, what jail is like (how did he know?), and finished by saying he would not call the police (the police?!) since it was my first—"and it better be your last, young lady"—offense.

❧

So clearly, I will have to step lightly regarding my newest footwear. If one lousy piece of stolen gum being chewed quietly can sound off alarms, imagine the questions about origin and ownership that my loud, clacking tap shoes will raise.

I feel exceptional carrying the shoes home. I discover the power of a prop. I am swinging the stunning shoes as I walk down my neighborhood streets, they catch in the sunlight and shine like a beacon to anyone who passes by or looks my way, they almost shout "Look! I am a dancer ... with official dancing shoes."

Finally at my driveway, I slip the rather snug shoes on, tie the black cotton ties (note to self, I need some purple or gold velvet ribbon) open the back door, walk in, and WOW! Instant Broadway musical! The spontaneous tapping, clicking, clacking on the linoleum turns our kitchen into the Radio City Music Hall, starring ...

"RONDA!"

My Rockettes' debut is stopped by my mother shouting, "What in the world are you doing?"

While it is quite clear I am dancing, I know better than to reply, "What does it look like I'm doing?"

Being a smart aleck or being perceived as the least bit disrespectful toward either our mother or father—even if at the same time you are showing some creativity and humor—did not justify the end result, the end usually being the rear end ...

Just last week my brother had answered the phone when my father called from work. He asked my brother what mother was up to and, to be cute, my brother sang the refrain from a popular song, "A Day in the Life of a Fool." I heard him and I laughed, I thought it was hilarious ... until I saw the blood drain from my brother's face and his body go soggy. I watched him slowly put the phone down, stumble to his room and gently shut the door. He stayed in there until my father came home and paid him a visit. I heard muffled voices, and the word "disrespectful" a number of times, along with, "So, you think you're a funny guy?" and the sounds of my brother crying. The memory of that visit and witnessing my brother's spine liquify was more than enough to back me away from being anything near disrespectful or funny about my mother's, let's be honest, pointless question ... as it was perfectly clear I was dancing.

❧

"Mother, I won a spot in the dance line for the school show. They passed out tap shoes for us to use, and guess what? I get to be a dancing elf!"

If I say I borrowed the shoes from Barbara, my mother will call Barb's parents to make sure it is OK that I have the shoes (trust level low after gum crime) and I can't risk the chance that Barbara has told her mother I can't afford tap shoes, I have sold them for meals, or anything close to that.

Creative license in my diary is one thing, but lying in real time is complicated business and demands I keep my wits about me at all times.

"Good for you," mother says, "just don't practice in here, you'll scuff the floors ... practice outside."

She doesn't say a word about the shoes! I click my heels together in a "there's no place like home" homage.

"No sweat," I say cheerfully, which turns out to be untrue, as practicing on the patio in the backyard in Phoenix is plenty sweaty. I don't care, I am dancing. Sort of. I am pure swelt, making lots of noise, my feet and arms moving furiously up, down, around, flap, step, flap ... my brother comes out and watches for a moment then walks away, disgusted, taunting me by saying, "You look like a praying mantis stuck in tar."

As my brother leaves, my mother comes out to join me. For a mesmerizing moment, on that shoddy, sandy patio she sashays, step-ball-changes, and chaisses back into her childhood. Spinning and twirling past me, she is the girl she once was, when dance lessons, singing at local cinemas, and entering beauty pageants held the promise of bigger and better things.

I have never seen this playful side of her, this smile, the laugh, the lilt. She suddenly is the suburban Juliet Prowse.

Until this moment, I have not seen my mother as anything but my mother, or to be more specific, someone married to my father. He is such a dominating presence, I never think of her as a separate person with dreams, hopes, quests and talents. As I watch her, I think maybe the high school picked the wrong person to honor with a fan club. I also see what she might have become if she wasn't stuck at home with us.

"I will teach you the Scottish jig," she declares with a jaunty wave of the hand and a cross over of the left foot, coming at a full tartan stop in front of me, her cheeks flushed and her auburn hair loosed.

"But I need to tap, not jig," I remind her.

"A jig, a tap, a waltz, it's all the same, just stand back, give me room, and watch my feet."

For the next few weeks I meet with her after school and we trip the patio fantastic. Sometimes we waltz, or do the Bossa Nova, the Charleston and the Lindy Hop. When she dances, she looks happy and content in a way that I have never seen until now.

My mother actually talks with me during these choreographed afternoons. She tells me that as a young girl she practiced dancing so much that she broke both of her arches and had to give it up. She admits that it was difficult having a divorced mother and says she didn't like having a stepfather. She had dreams of dancing through life, and shares in-depth details about the dashing of those dreams that sounds jarringly familiar to me. Her story, in fact, with the names and faces changed, could be my story. She, too, felt special and destined for something undefined, but great.

This bit of revelation is far from comforting.

If I don't mind my steps, my throat constricts at the mere thought, I, too, might have a baby seven years from now, marry someone because I think he is cute, and spend my afternoons waiting for him to get home.

I practice the dancing elf routine hour after hour, day after day. Blisters, ingrown toenails, bloody heels, broken capillaries, and family heckling don't deter me. Already skinny, I begin to lose weight from the perpetual motion I am in. My mother and father watch me rehearse one afternoon. My mother tells my father that because of all my dancing I have lost at least ten pounds.

He considers this and then says to me, "Look behind you."

My diligence pays off. I am selected lead dancer in the "Frosty the Snowman" extravaganza of the Orangewood Elementary Holiday Pageant. Jimmy Carson might be the snowman, but that night I am the showman. I own the stage, out-performing the other fairies, as well as Frosty, tapping to the beat of my happy, happy heart.

Though I revel in the applause and momentary appreciation of being the star of the show, the next day I return Barbara Cadkin's taps.

I do not want to step into someone else's shoes. The Dance badge has left me feeling even more determined to fill my own.

Math is used everywhere ... become a math whiz
and you can do anything.

GIRL SCOUT BADGE BOOK

Math Whiz

The only time in my life when I don't feel like a math bird-
brain, I win a parakeet.

I am sitting on the couch in my aunt's living room and her
parakeet flies to my shoulder, nuzzles my hair, and sips
from the glass of Coke I am holding. Pete the parakeet and
I are birds of a feather and I desperately want one. We love
the same drink, we sing for anyone who will listen, and our
wings keep getting clipped. After years of not budging, one
afternoon my father tires of my pleading for a bird of my
own and suggests a wager.

"What is a wager?" I ask.

"Go look it up," my father responds, thus buying himself a
few more moments of being left alone.

He always tells us to look words up and I always argue, "if I don't know how to spell it, how can I look it up?" He never offers us a clue or gives us a hint. Sometimes we won't be seen for days as we pathetically turn page by page in the dictionary, forgoing meals or watching *Have Gun–Will Travel* as we search for words like ptomaine poison or xylophone.

"A wager: to risk or bet money or property on the outcome of a game, event, or uncertain situation," I read to him after a relatively brief word reconnaissance mission of twenty minutes.

"Use it in a sentence," he taunts.

"I will wager my brother for a parakeet," I try.

"No, that would be a fair trade," he says. "There is an element of risk in a wager, you could lose something, or you have a chance to win something. Try again."

"I just want a parakeet," I whine, "not a dog, not a bike, just a bird ... and I bet you are going to say no."

"Good, that's closer. Tell you what I am going to do. I will make you a wager and you could win a parakeet."

"Will I lose something?" I ask, beginning to not like the sounds of wager.

"Go get me some dice," he continues.

This is just another obvious ploy for more peace and quiet. We rarely play board games together so "go get some dice" is a request he often makes like, "go play on the freeway." He imagines, no, hopes, I might never return.

Like the determined and resourceful scout I am, I'm back in an instant with Yahtzee dice from some Christmas past.

My father is surprised by my speed, but remains calm, as he takes the dice from me and explains the rules of a game called Craps. There's lots of talking about points, odds, and combinations. He is on a roll, and keeps talking, but all I hear is:

"If you get a seven on your first throw, *I will get you a parakeet and cage, everything you need to own a bird.* If it's anything else, any other number besides seven, you lose and cannot ask for a bird of any kind again for the rest of your life."

He looks right at me, daring me with a gaze that implies "put up or shut up." He had the same look one afternoon when I chose a spanking over a nap, and even though the spanking was to be with a fly swatter, I had gambled his heart wouldn't be in it. I was betting he couldn't spank me hard if I hadn't really done anything wrong ... and I turned out to be right. It was a few taps of the wire mesh swatter and I got stay up to watch *Wizard of Oz* without having to take a nap.

Maybe I am a good wager-er after all.

"I'm in!" I cry out, flush with the exhilaration of the ignorant and then I shush, careful not to allow myself to get to the point of ebullient ...

In our house, we always had to be cautious about how excited any of us got over activities, or good news, or special events. For example, I was told to leave the room when I watched the news and then cried about President Kennedy being shot.

"Why are you crying?" my father demanded, "you didn't know him."

If we made too much noise, or got too happy, too sad, or too involved, my father was likely to halt whatever was going on right then and there.

Take for example the *Flintstones*, premiere. The first animated night-time television show was national news and the entire country was planning on watching it. My mother got into the spirit and made a festive evening out of the occasion. She bought all us kids a TV tray, she purchased Swanson's frozen dinners, she even poured us Hi-C to drink instead of milk. This was a BIG NIGHT. At the appointed hour we were perched in front of the set, behind our trays, and as the theme song started, *Flintstones, meet the Flintstones, they're the modern stone-age family* we were overcome by the hoopla and hype, and probably the red dye in the punch, and began waving our forks in the sky and yelling "Yabba-Dabba-Do" at the top of our lungs. We were living it up—laughing, jumping up and down, eating frozen chicken dinners, and swilling our drinks—when out of nowhere my father walked past us, straight to the television set, and turned it off. Emphatically turned it off, with dictatorial flamboyance.

"They're just excited, let them watch the show," my mother appealed.

He turned to look at us, each by now stone quiet, the gravel-like peas from our frozen dinner protruding through our cheeks, "One more chance, keep it quiet in here or it goes off for good."

"Yes, sir," we replied in a hushed unison ... and then as he left the living room my brother whispered, "and Yabba-Dabba-Do to you, too," which cracked us quietly up.

Therefore, it is imperative that I remain calm, and I do so

as my father stands up and clears a space in the living room for our game of chance. He moves the coffee table aside and backs the occasional chair against the wall. One of us sits in that chair every day, not occasionally. And no one ever drinks coffee at that table. And believe me, our so-called living room is really our "you are banished" room. Words, I consider—although I love them—can be confusing, they can be daunting, words can get you grounded or worse. But numbers, although I have previously disdained them, can win me a pet.

I am getting more interested in math by the minute.

"You can blow on the dice, you can wish for a seven out loud, you can do a little skip before you throw, whatever you want to do, baby! You must make the dice talk to you!"

Now it is my father who is flushed, oddly animated, and boisterous about the whole process. I get caught up in his revelry and we dance around the room as I shake the dice in my hand, which I hold high above my head. One of us is heading for disaster, but at the moment we are both on the same side—the side of suspense, anticipation, and fun. All the hubbub is going to my head and I find myself laughing and hiccupping at the same time.

By now the hollering has attracted the attention of the rest of my family and they slowly gather around me as I finally squat knee deep in the shag carpet ready to gamble for avian destiny.

Big, important moments in life—that is to say, usually the bad or potentially bad stuff—seem to happen in slow motion. Case in point: when I was run over by a bike ridden by the neighbor boy who dared me to cross the street. I remember seeing his mouth curl sluggishly into a snarl, I recall deliberately turning my head and forcing my suddenly heavy eyelids open to make eye contact with him before the impact. I felt each of my ribs come into contact with the handle bars, felt each vertebrae in my neck stretch to the far right, could feel the squish of each tread as the tires kerplumped over my hips and legs. The hit and run felt like it lasted twenty minutes. My brother, however—who was sitting and cheering from the sidelines—said later it looked like our home movies on fast forward and that my attacker should be congratulated on his velocity and aim. "It actually takes a certain degree of skill to run over a person and not fall off the bike yourself," he said with respect.

My roll of the dice, the unity of my family whooping, wondering if I will roll a seven, my glance upward at the silhouette of my father against the living room window, the dream of my own Petey bird on my shoulder, the episode seems everlasting. The dice writhe and ramble and stumble through the loops and lengths of the weed-high carpet and finally tip and topple as the first one comes slowly to rest as a six. I cover my eyes, not able to watch what the second die will do, the crowd becomes hushed and finally I hear my father whisper, "I'll be damned." I open one eye and squint at the solitary back dot on the remaining die. We all hang in suspended animation for what feels like the entire afternoon until finally my father says, "Guess you better name your bird Craps."

Although earning my Girl Scout badges is vital to my campaign for immortality; my efforts to become famous, or gifted, or a memoirist, a singer, or a dancer are so far adding up to zero. I clearly need to broaden my skill set and discover other avenues of achievement. My resounding win in statistical probability and odds landed me the parakeet I named Tinkerbell and with the thrill of victory pushing me onward, I commit to playing the numbers game for my next badge.

It will be the toughest hurdle for me yet.

I appreciate that the letters of the alphabet mean something when you put them together. Reading a good book can make me laugh or cry and with words I can make a friend, sing a song, and even compose poems, like the one I write for my parakeet shortly after winning her:

"I have a little bird
Her name is Tinkerbell
And every time I look at her
I tell her she is swell
I feed her in the morning
And I talk to her at night
And when I put my finger in
I'm sure to get a bite."

And, speaking of letters, I get an "A" for that rhyme!

Some schools use a number for grades, yuck. I like seeing that "A" on a paper, it would not be nearly as impressive to see a number "1."

I find numbers cold, stiff, and lacking in all humor and individuality. There is only one right answer to a math question. I find this incredibly boring. I know some of my classmates are charmed by this exactitude and stability, but these are the same classmates who would never have cried while watching *Old Yeller* unless the movie had a scene in which Yeller scratches his age in the dirt with his paw.

Many teachers try to convince me of the value of math. Even so, I can't get myself to care how much wallpaper a room of mine would need.

One, because I usually don't live in a house long enough to notice if the wallpaper needs changing and two, because I know if and when the day comes and I have my own home to wallpaper, I will hire someone good at math and handy with glue to do it. And when I am grown up, it will be my chauffeur who calculates how long a car trip will take and how many miles per gallon my Rolls Royce gets.

Nope. Wallpaper, miles per gallon—my interest rate for most of the uses of math is nil. I need a better reason or a higher call to care about math than what school gives me or what badge requirements can inspire.

Providence intervenes and my badgering becomes crucial to a cause I can get behind, national security.

The Russians put a man in a rocket and launched him to outer space. To add insult to injury, he makes it back to earth alive. America has lost to the Russians? This is not to be tolerated and schools throughout our great country are told to teach students more math and science so we can trounce communism back to where it belongs ... which I guess is out of space and back to Russia.

Before their successful whipping of America, Russians were only mentioned in school during bomb drills. Once a week we were forced under our flimsy metal desks with the wood laminate writing surface, hands over our heads and eyes closed in case the "Ruskies drop a bomb."

Even I know that being under a small wooden desk, staring at the scuff marks on the well-trod floor (that my nose is smushed against) while using my measly arm muscles to shield my head will barely save me from a spit wad, let alone an atom bomb.

At least it's a few moments of peace and quiet, allowing me to ponder my place in the world and this place called the world. A few questions burble in my un-safeguarded head while these moments spent cramped in a huddle plod by:

1. Why does my teacher grab her purse before diving under her desk? What in heaven's name is in that bag that is necessary to have when she is blown to bits?

2. Why are we always arranged alphabetically? Will I really have to die next to Margo Axsom?

3. What do the Russian's have against us elementary school students anyway?

Laying under the desk, I calculate my place value thusly; reading the most books, spelling the most words correctly, winning contests, and accepting awards will be what makes my blown-to-bits life matter. If my diary is unearthed, like Anne Frank, maybe I will be remembered and celebrated for my goodwill toward mankind ... note to self, put more goodwill toward mankind stuff in diary.

Since I want to live a long life, I do not relish the thought of being blown to smithereens on a cheap floor, and because math is the way to conquer the "red menace," prove my patriotism, and stick to my pledge to "serve God and my country," plus knowing I need to explore other activities for both my badges and my betterment, it is only logical to become a Math Whiz.

And this is how and why, in the fourth grade, I become Arizona's, and possibly the nation's, highest scorer on the national math IQ test.

The math curriculum has been revised to include "new math," which must be meant to help us communicate with the aliens we will meet when we do get to outer space.

I am not good at the new math, in fact it is too new for the teachers to be good at it. By the time of the statewide IQ test I know how to get the wrong answer in both Base Six and Base Ten, which is like Base Six if you are missing four fingers. In addition, I am attending the third different school for my fourth grade and unpacking my stuff in the third house of that year.

The odds of me doing well in my nightly math homework are not great, let alone scoring highly in a statewide aptitude exam.

The way I figure my chances is if x=IQ test and y=math comprehension and you divide that by 4 x3 representing my grade level times the number of classrooms and houses I have been in and add negative twenty for loss of friends, the sum total is < IQ score but = my probability of doing well in a math IQ exam, whether it is in new or old math.

When the test is administered, I have been a fourth grader at Osborne Elementary for a week. I am escorted to the class by another in a long line of dark suited principals, introduced to my classmates with feigned sincerity by a frazzled teacher, and keep my chin up as whispers and stifled laughter from the other students sweep the room. The introduction is followed by the scraping of a spare desk along the floor by the biggest or plumpest boy in class. Then an entire row of desks is reconnoitered as mine is wedged, usually in alphabetical order, up front.

I have been the new kid in school so many times that I have the routine down to a science. I expect no one to look at me for the entire morning and I keep my eyes on the clock above the blackboard, a smile pasted on my face. Bearing this slight elevated and jutted profile, I imagine, makes me look like I am waiting for Jesus to come save me. Recess is spent walking around the playground doing field research. For survival I need to determine who is good at tetherball, who owns the four square court, who is a bully and who is an outcast. Outcasts have no other friends, so they are always the first to talk to me. This is a fragile union. I appreciate the outsiders, but if I become their friend too steadfastly, I become not only the new student, I am the new AND exiled student. Nothing about the formula is easy, no matter how many times I do it.

At lunchtime, I sit alone in the cafeteria or pretend to be walking home. Then, rather than go home, I eat my peanut better sandwich as I sit on a curb, in some neighborhood, close to school.

By the afternoon, some of the stranger danger in class wears off and someone with a desk close to me lends me a pencil, or tells me what page we are on in an assignment. Once verbal contact has been made, I take that opportunity and try to build what I already know will be a passing friendship from it. Most of my friends throughout my school days are the kids who eat their boogers, wear thick glasses, have a limp, or kids who have last names that start with A or B.

My first friend at Osborne Elementary fits both categories. Wesley Abbott, who looks a little like a young, beardless version of Mr. French, the butler from the television show, *Family Affair,* passes a handout to me and we bond over the warmth and smell of the mimeographed papers being distributed by the teacher, Mrs. Barnes.

He takes a deep whiff, his nose flat against the stack, and says,

"If there are any extras I'll eat them."

Mrs. Barnes announces at the end of the day, "tomorrow we have America's Math Proficiency Exam. Get to bed early."

"I just got here," I say smugly, "I don't even know what that test is. I don't think she will make me take it."

"We all have to take it," Wesley tells me as we leave the classroom and pass through the door marked "Barnes Door" "we've been studying all month."

"I have been studying math since first grade and have decided I am a great speller," I say to Wesley, not thrilled by my welcome gift of a critical exam, and in math, no less, but thankful I have a buddy.

The next day, as I sit in my assigned seat in my IQ class doom, Wesley swaggers to his desk, like only fourth grade boys can, and tells me,

"My dad told me this test is no big deal, I know as much math as any fourth grader."

"My father told me that everyone has an IQ, even me," I reply, and am not surprised that Wesley doesn't laugh. I didn't either.

Mrs. Barnes takes roll, passes each of us a thick pad of papers as she issues the ominous, teacher-is-passing-out-a-serious-test-warning, "don't turn this over until I say so," while looking directly at each of us with that universal teacher stink-eye-squinty-look that they use to convey "I mean business."

Yep, for sure, this exam must be of national interest.

At 9:00 a.m. the loudspeaker positioned above the clock and to the right of the portrait of Abe Lincoln crackles to life:

"Boys and Girls, today is an important day in your life. Today will determine your aptitude for mathematics, your possible future careers, and your abilities to be productive members of our great nation."

I start to panic. Geez, can't dance, can't sing, can't math. What's to become of me I think, and then begin to fiddle with the stack of papers on my desk. Lincoln had to scratch his arithmetic in dirt, he read by candlelight, and despite this he becomes President. I have paper, I have electricity, and what good is it doing me? I continue to berate myself and tinker with my exam.

By now the principal has signed off, wishing us luck and Mrs. Barnes is barking out the instructions.

"You are to use your pencil," she says. "Read each question and color in the circle that marks your answer. You have one hour until the first break."

My head is down, my hands clammy and twitchy, my thumb moving up and down rapidly on the papers before me when I notice, feel actually, something loose ... underneath the test sheet ... it's, what ... huh? Carbon paper? I pull the exam a little further apart. Under the carbon paper there is another sheet of paper with the circles already blacked in ... what is this? It's the key? The answers are attached to the back of the test!

I look right to left, all my classmates have their heads down, pencils gripped, working furiously on the test. Up front, the teacher is sitting at her desk reading the morning paper.

I continue to pull very carefully until I can see the entire answer key.

The keys to the kingdom, the answers to each question, the solution to my compound problem is right in front of me, well, right under the test in front of me.

I can only say in my defense it must be patriotic fervor, or maybe the stress of being new at this school, perhaps a desperate cry for attention or simply momentary insanity, but whatever it is, it compels me to not just fill in a few right answers. I fill them all in correctly, every last question on the first part of the exam. Then Parts Two and Three later that day. All of the fractions, the angles, the obtuse and degree, the hypotenuse and circumference, every single question answered correctly without me even reading the questions. As I color in the right circle, time after time, I feel giddy, I feel powerful, I feel brilliant. I have out-maneuvered all the smart people who put together this lame exam. Me, a lowly, multi-moved fourth grader, can crack the code. I clearly have aptitudes school isn't meas-uring. Maybe I can be an astronaut! Or a spy!

At the end of the arduous testing day my fellow students are spent from so much concentration and sitting. I, however, literally skip home. I feel good. I have bested the exam, it is over, I am finished and I finished well. I eat a hearty dinner, volunteer to do dishes, and go to bed.

Dear Diary, I write before turning out the lights, *Did well in state math test, 100 percent. Perhaps I will build a rocket and give poor children a ride to Mars*, I finish, thinking of Anne Frank.

How is it that I can lie in my diary, lie about knowing how to play piano, steal gum, lie myself into lead elf, and cheat on a national exam all the while pledging as a scout that I will be honest and fair?

The truth is, I don't have a carbon key that can answer that question.

Everything I do, when I do it, is simply part of my crusade to get somewhere better, be someone special, and at the time I think that what I am doing is merely stepping in the right direction.

I'm not hurting anyone, I'm advancing myself, is what I subconsciously think. In my day-to-day life, I am like a walking, talking pinball game. If I hit a detour or get paddled, if I end up in the wrong tunnel or on the opposite side, if I hear bells or whistles I re-route without thinking about anything except staying in the game, getting the most action from my turn, and winning.

By Friday of the test week, I am a little late for school because during breakfast my father is filling out my doctor release forms for sports and he is taking his sweet time. He finishes the release, has me look up "Physicians" in the yellow pages, and asks me to read some names to him until he finds one he likes. He signs, "Dr. Jeff Alred." We have been through this drill a number of times. At each new school, as a matter of fact. And I know from past experience—like the time I told him that I had an earache and he proceeded to blow cigarette smoke in my ear and say it was a Navajo way to ease pain—that it doesn't matter what name is on the school health form, or what is wrong with me, my father will always be my doctor.

With consent in hand, I whisk through the "Barnes Door" and slide into my seat just as the public address system comes on.

Wesley signals "Safe" and we laugh while the principle clears his throat, broadcasting "Attention, attention students," then pauses and begins what he says is a "very thrilling and important message."

"Girls and Boys, I am proud to announce to you this morning that Osborne Elementary School is home to the top fourth grade math student in the state."

Everyone, including me, is looking around the room wondering who this prodigy could possibly be. Some students are clapping, some are whooping, I am enjoying the energy in the room, ready to celebrate with the smart son-of-a gun. This could mean a party instead of the regularly scheduled show-and-tell, I hope not wanting to sit through more displays of souvenirs from Disneyland, photos of pets, favorite stuffed toys, or Milk Duds that have melted into the shape of a barnyard animal.

"In fact," the announcement continues, "this is a new student at Osborne, and we are delighted she is here and putting us on the map."

In my defense, there are two other fourth grades, so I am still waiting to hear the name of this math whiz when the principal's voice cries out, "RONDA BEAMAN."

Classmates are patting me on the back, Wesley Abbot's head whips around to look at me in utter amazement, and my teacher covers her mouth with both hands to stifle, what? A scream? A howl? A laugh?

No matter, in my just announced mathematically magical brain I am flat lining, no sign of life. Dead head.

Better get me to the doctor … oh wait, remembering the sports release form, better not.

My brain is drained but my nervous system, oh man, my whole body is alive with raw, trembling terror.

The class quickly settles down. Fame is fleeting in the fourth grade and is easily replaced by more pressing matters of the day, like the Pledge of Allegiance or a spelling test.

Mrs. Barnes approaches my desk before letting us out for recess and asks me to remain after school to speak with her about my math IQ results before I walk home.

I spend recess hidden in the third stall of the girls pink tiled bathroom, feet up off the floor so no one can see me. I need to think, and think fast. I sit on the toilet, my head resting on my knees and consider my options. What if the school has already contacted my parents with the Big News?

No, we don't have a phone hooked up yet.

So far, so good.

And worse yet, what if this incident has made the papers?

This is not delusions of grandeur on my part. Just last year I was the headline story on the front page of the *Arizona Republic* ...

"State Book Float Winner Loves Jungle Doctor" ran the entire width of the paper and featured a big photo of my smiling face underneath it, grinning ear-to-ear and holding the molten remains of my float entry in the parade. I won the Blue Ribbon fair and square for reading a book about Albert Schweitzer and then, with strict adherence to the rules, creating a transportable diorama to depict a scene from the book.

Many kids, by the looks of the floats on contest day, had not read the rules, which specifically stated that you had to build your own float. There were jeweled castle floats, three feet high, constructed from balsa wood and forming cathedral like spires. There were motorized floats with gears and shifts, erupting volcano floats, and even floats big enough to hold parents in costumes playing characters from their child's favorite book.

Not all kids had help from adults ... my brother and I, as well as a few others, were obvious Do-It-Your-selfers. For the most part, with the exception being me, these were the kids who didn't read books, didn't want to do a float, and only participated because their teachers made them do it. They were not contenders. My brother, for example, put a piece of drywall on a skate, placed a plastic turtle on top and *Voilà!*—Tommy the Turtle Book Float.

Once I saw the magnitude of professionalism and parental intercession I was up against, I didn't think I had a chance to win anything other than my Book Badge.

My float was a garbage can lid that I had filled with gravel. I then stuck small branches of eucalyptus trees in clumps of modeling clay to depict a jungle and I painted my brother's plastic Civil War soldiers black to represent the natives. I set them under the trees or entering the hut I had made from a sawed in half coconut shell. I saved one soldier and painted him white and put some cotton on his head to look like Dr. Schweitzer. I was pretty proud of my village, until I saw what the other kids, I mean, what the other kids' parents had done.

Nonetheless, I dragged my garbage lid, tied to a piece of rope, down the parade path. I was a shoe-in for noisiest float, or float that scratches the sidewalk. While waiting to be judged, my clay started to melt in the 100 degree heat and the jungle trees kept falling over. I was propping trees up with gravel and relieving my cotton topped Dr. Schweitzer by placing him under some shade as the official judge stepped up to my float.

He had a camera around his neck, a pencil behind his ear, and a notepad in his hand. He wore glasses that reflected the brutal sun and my sweaty and serious face. "What have you got here?" he asked like someone who had already heard the answer to the question too many times.

I proceeded to tell him not about my float, or the melting clay, or how hard it was for me to saw the coconut in half and make it look like a hut. I chose not to apologize for the tiny bayonets and muskets the black natives were holding or mention the large scrape marks the garbage can lid left on the sidewalks, but I did tell him about Albert Schweitzer.

"Dr. Schweitzer left his home and country, left everything he knew and loved, to start a hospital in the deepest jungles. It was the first hospital in Africa. And, he not only built it, he was the doctor who treated all these people. He also taught them to read. He earned money to do this by playing organs at churches. He never got married or had his own family because he was so dedicated to helping people no one else was helping. He just felt someone had to help them and he did it. If everyone was like Dr. Schweitzer, the world would be a much better place," I finished.

And, I won. I was front page news not because my float was the best, it wasn't. I won because the judge could tell I had learned something of value from the book and he chose me because I followed the rules and I had done the work myself.

Well, I did this math exam work all by myself, too, and I won first place again. But I didn't follow the rules and there's no way—me with by burgeoning badge collection— that I can say I didn't know this was cheating. I did know, and I did it anyway. What do they do to state IQ cheaters? I shudder as I imagine group homes where disappointed parents drop off their larcenous young, or prisons filled with other elementary grade offenders who are forced to exist on green vegetables and wear one-piece jumpsuits with a Sansa-Belt.

Or worse, put your picture in the paper as First Prize cheat.

My restroom recess ends, I hop off the toilet, straighten out my numb legs and walk back to class, praying there will be no newspaper reporter available today. I hope we move again, I think. Like, tomorrow.

The day lingers and my dread continues to mount with each tick of the second hand on the clock. It doesn't help that the gaze from the portrait of Honest Abe now seems to be directed only at me.

The final bell rings and everyone bolts for home while I remain planted at my desk. I remain there while Mrs. Barnes erases the board and begins chattily to tell me what lie in store for me.

"Why, Ronda, you must be very excited. This single event could change your life."

"You have no idea," I reply faintly, thinking that fainting right now might be the way to go.

Mrs. Barnes puts down the eraser and gathers some papers from her desk.

"Come with me," she extends her hand. I grab it and stand up to walk with her. "We are going to the principal's office to make arrangements for you to be on a bus daily, after lunch, to a trip to Central High School. Doesn't that sound fun?"

"I guess, but what for?" I am thinking that high school may be where the prison is.

"Well, Ronda," Mrs. Barnes says as we amble down the breezeway hand in hand, "we don't have the teachers or the time to teach you the type of math someone of your caliber needs.

Like the Calculus-of-Coming-Clean? my brain silently chimes in. But I reply, "What kind do I need?"

"Oh, algebra, geometry, trigonometry, statistics, the usual."

She may as well be speaking a foreign language and I feel my hand go clammy in hers and hope Mrs. Barnes doesn't notice.

"If you do as well as we think you will, you will soon go to Arizona State University to study with other gifted students."

This is becoming dreadful, but it isn't over. As we approach the principal's office, the staff announces my arrival with a "State Champ! State Champ!" cheer. The principal quickly stands up from his desk as we enter and salutes me. He salutes!

"Ronda, we are so proud of you. We are planning an assembly to give you a plaque and let you tell the rest of the school how fun math is and maybe we'll start a math club and you can be the first president ..." I see his mouth continue to spew out his plans for my coronation, but I hear nothing except my inner math tutor telling me that I had better subtract myself from this equation pronto.

I begin to cry.

"Now, now, dear," Mrs. Barnes puts her arm around me, "it's all a little overwhelming, we know. But we'll make sure you have fun just being a fourth grader, too."

Now I accelerate into wailing and heaving and sobbing uncontrollably.

"I can't do it!" I yell between sobs. "I just can't do it."

"Do what? No one is going to make you do anything. We can call your parents and we can all work out a good plan for you ... we can work together ..."

"NO! Please don't call my parents, please."

The principal pulls up a chair for me, he looks concerned as he helps me sit down. Mrs. Barnes hands me a Kleenex and puts her hand on my shoulder. They are both standing above me and I am looking at the floor when, without even planning to, I blurt and blubber, "I cheated."

"Yes, dear, yes you did beat it. You were perfect! You are perfect" Mrs. Barnes says, mistaking my malady and shaking her head sadly at the principal.

"No, I *cheee*-ted." I pronounce it clearly this time, "I cheated on the IQ test. I am no math whiz, I am no genius, I am no one"... and with that I collapse and continue crying, my hands covering my face, ashamed to be seen by them, not wanting to see them.

For the next hour, in the small and disheveled office of an undistinguished administrator and with the help of a middle-aged fourth grade teacher I learn the explicit function of honesty, as well as the absolute value of compassion, and the vector of transformation.

After my confession detailing how I picked the papers apart and found the answers, and sniveling through the tale of my many moves to different schools, and weeping my apology and more begging to please, please not tell my parents, the principal and the teacher look down on me and are silent.

This is the first time I have ever spilled my guts to anyone, it is the first time I show any vulnerability or fear, or even admit any to myself. It is my first taste of self inflicted failure.

And in the stillness, in what should be a moment of relief, I feel ... I feel ... shoddy. As if not only am I nothing special—

I am nothing, period. A null and void.

As I look up at my superiors, I see in their eyes ... pity.

They feel sorry for me and this only adds to the disgust and shame flowing through my veins.

The principal finally says,

"You are right, Ronda, this was a wrong thing to do, and when members of our school, or our society, do something wrong, there are consequences."

"Yes, sir."

I believe nothing he thinks of will be worse for me than the punishment of this moment.

Mrs. Barnes says sadly, "I know it must be tough on you to be the new student, but cheaters never prosper."

Yuck.

Up until now, all the stories I have told and falsehoods I have propagated have been relatively harmless, if you don't count stealing the Juicy Fruit gum. And, in my mind, all of them were necessary.

But, I have gone too far this time. I am in the national champs of liars and cheaters. And I realize I better change my answers to the question of who I really want to be and how I am going to get there.

The principal and Mrs. Barnes will not tell my parents, they say, and nothing further is mentioned to my classmates. My punishment is to stay after school for the rest of the year to tutor any second or third graders who need extra help in arithmetic.

I am relieved by the reprimand and promise to make them proud of me again someday.

I move to another school two weeks later.

This time, though—packed along with my clothes, toys, and parakeet—I take a recently discovered equation. If I am ever going to be an integer, that is whole, I need to learn to divide my aspirations by my aptitudes. Being a Math Whiz helps me figure out that using a fraction of the truth to get what I want will only subtract from, not multiply, my accomplishments.

Whether you are a budding entrepreneur
or prefer to help out from the sidelines,
you can learn a lot when it comes to cookies!

GIRL SCOUT BADGE BOOK

The Cookie Connection

I am sitting at the table of the Girl Scout awards dinner waiting impatiently to receive my merit badges and various other honors I have accrued.

After a couple of these dinners my troop leader finally just got me a seat up on the stage. This way I don't have to keep the audience waiting while I bounce up the aisle when my name is called.

"This evening's award for Most Effective Patrol Leader belongs to ..."

Ronda Beaman.

"The Photography Badge is earned by ..."

Ronda Beaman.

"Tonight's award for Most Visits to the Nursing Home goes to ..."

Ronda Beaman.

It is a re-run evening for everyone else, my parent's never even bother to come, but I love every moment. I become Ronda Beam*ing*.

It is because I have this tradition of excess to uphold that, at this year's cookie selling season, I naturally sign up to sell the most cases.

I smile as I sign on the dotted line for sixty cases of Do-si-dos, Shortbread Trefoils, and Thin Mints. I am confident I can move this much product, even cocky, and I enjoy the eyes of all the girls in the troop on me as balance and drag my cases home. The awe with which they stepped aside to let me pass was like the respect I witnessed on the news as the workers at Cape Canaveral watched astronaut John Glenn walk toward his rocket for take-off. Like our first man in space, I am pushing the envelope and exploring new frontiers.

I plan to be among the stars of cookie sales.

On the morning of sales day I prepare myself with a good breakfast, treat my hair to a wash with eucalyptus scented shampoo, don a crisp uniform, slip into my highly polished shoes, grab my white gloves, and wear my usual happy attitude. With my bow tie (embossed with the Girl Scout insignia) secured in place, as well as my badge-populated sash across my chest, I leave my room singing my version of a Girl Scout standard I learned as a Brownie, *"I've got something in my pocket that belongs across my face, I keep it very close at hand, in a most convenient place ..."* I skip into the living room to pick up my six crates of cookies. *"I'm sure you couldn't guess it, if you guessed a long, long, while ..."* I continue, passing my brother and sister with a regulation two-finger salute. They don't even bother to look at me because both are glued to Saturday morning cartoons. Although tempted to join them and watch my favorite, "Fractured Fairy Tales" and Mr. Peabody the talking dog, I keep my bigger mission in mind and sashay myself toward the kitchen.

Even though I had inspected and prepped my cartons of cookies the night before, I decide to check my product yet again, to ensure my Thin Mints are easier to access than the Shortbread. Mints are the big movers; every scout knows that. Save the shortbread cookies for the nursing home stop.

"So I'll take it out and put it on, it's a great big cookie selling smile."

"WHAT the heck?" my singing and smiling end when I spy a small, meticulous slit, covered by a piece of cellophane tape, on a box of my Thin Mints. My first thought is that the troop leader has given me a used box of cookies. I hadn't caught it last night, but in the dawn's early light, the box shows the signs of being opened.

Upon closer inspection, though, the box has not just been opened. It has been tampered with by an expert ... a madman ... or both. There are no tatters and no ragged edges. The break-in has the kind of attention to detail that fills me with admiration ... while making my skin crawl at the same time.

I pull out another box and see the same cut, in the same place, covered up by using the same tape.

Another box. And another. And another. I start tearing through the multiple boxes of cookies trusted to me to sell that day and find every single box has been opened in the identical manner and re-sealed in the very same corner. All sixty boxes. The forced cookie box entry had to take hours of painstaking and diabolical work. Someone hunched over my cases of cookies and opened each one … but why? And when?

I tear off the tape, open a box, and find two cookies missing. I open another—two cookies missing. Two cookies have been removed from every box? One hundred and twenty cookies stolen? The villain is not only able to focus for long periods of time, he or she has a colossal sweet tooth.

I run to my father screaming hysterically and clutching a box of opened cookies in each hand, "During the night someone broke into my cookies, they are all open, every single box is ruined!"

"Stop the dramatics, there's no possible way every box of cookies is open," he grunts. He puts down his paper, snuffs out his cigarette, and reluctantly moseys to my cookie box rubble. He grabs a box and inspects it, holding it up to the light and turning it over a few times. He tosses that one aside and lifts another box, and then another, picking up speed as he goes, finally throwing the last one to me.

"Did you do this?" he snarls accusingly.

"Me??? Why would I do this to my own cookies? I am supposed to sell these today, my chance of winning the Best Sales Pin is over," I sob.

"That's the exact reason it might be you, no one would suspect you."

"What? You can't be serious," I cry, but I can see he is plenty serious and suspicious. "Daddy, I did not steal my own cookies. It has to be someone else in this house, I checked all of the boxes last night before I went to bed and everything was fine."

I pretty much know my mother didn't do it, she would ante up the dollar for a box of her own, or my father would advance it to her. My parakeet Tinkerbell would never tape each box up that well, and my father doesn't like cookies because cookies don't go well with scotch.

It has to be my brother or sister.

My father stares at me amidst the pile of cookies while my mother comes over and sifts through the cartons. She then calls what I know to be the culprits—my siblings—to come to the kitchen. They come wandering in looking innocent, quizzical even, a dumb "what's happening?" type of look on each of their faces as they stumble toward the sprawl of ruined cookie boxes.

Oh, look at them, so above suspicion ... they are good, they are very good. I think, holding back my urge to shake and scratch them both with all my might until they 'fess up.

"Which one of you ripped open all my cookies? Who ate my cookies?" I run up to each of them like a bloodhound, sniffing for the smell of chocolate or peanut butter, getting close enough to see any telltale crumbs in the corners of their mouths. "You'll pay for this, I'll find out and you'll pay," I threaten with my little white-gloved fist.

"Alright you three," my father interjects, "line up against this wall."

"Why do I have to line up?" I cry, "I am the victim here, the victim isn't in the line up." Hasn't he seen enough of Sgt. Joe Friday on *Dragnet* to know how to handle a crime scene?

"I said all three of you against the wall, and that includes you Little Miss Merit Badge."

My father often calls us "The Good, The Bad, and The Ugly," but we never know which one of us is which. Except for today. Today, I know for certain I am the Good. But I still have to get against the wall because my father believes we are guilty until proven innocent.

Standing with our backs against the kitchen-wall-line-up is me, in full regulation scout regalia, my brother in Lone Ranger and Tonto pajamas and my sister in Lady and the Tramp t-shirt and shorts.

My father, serving as both judge and jury, lays out the case of the missing cookies. According to him each of us has a past record of petty larceny, a motive, and no alibi.

"You were all in the house last night, you all had the opportunity, and you all like cookies," he says, pacing slowly past us still wearing his baby blue shorty robe.

No one should see their father in a shorty anything.

"So, I am going to give the person responsible for this crime a chance to speak up, and if no one admits it, you will all three suffer the consequences."

"This is so unfair," I retort, "I am already in trouble for having all these boxes of cookies that are un-sellable. That's my punishment."

"Oh, they're sold, you can be sure of that, to all three of you, unless someone admits their guilt."

"There is no reason for the thief to admit it," I plead, "if we all have to pay, instead of the crook paying alone, why would anyone admit they're guilty?"

"Because whoever did this may not want the innocent among you to suffer."

Where has my father been all these years and what children has he been dealing with for the past decade?

"This is insane!" I screech.

"Insanity is a good plea," my brother chirps looking sideways at me and stifling a laugh, the corners of his mouth inching up.

That's when I know the fresh-faced boy wearing the masked-man pajamas is the cookie bandit.

I stare at him and, as they say happens just before you die, our short history passes before my eyes. My brother and I have a precarious relationship at best, and a hostile one at worst. Actions speak louder than words and whether dumping a boulder on my head, or shooting me with a dart gun, his actions scream "die!" or, at the very least, disappear permanently with no forwarding address.

The battles between my brother and I are often Biblical in proportions. I am convinced that someday my name will be in lights and his face will be on the Most Wanted poster at the post office along with other brothers who pitch hardballs at their sisters, hit them with fly swatters, tie jump ropes around their ankles and pull them around the carport, or put pickle juice in their chocolate milk and insect repellent in their perfume bottles. He engineers a path of destruction through my life whenever and however he can ...

Some classmates gave me a gold embossed **"Address Book"** for a moving away party in my honor two houses ago. It was filled with their names, addresses, and warm sentiments about how much they would miss me. My brother got a hold of it, scratched out the tender and generous expressions, and covered them in black marker that read "I'm glad you're leaving" and "You're too ugly to be missed," and my all time favorite, "Your brother is a cool dude." I ran into his room, waving the address book and screaming that this time he had gone too far.

"I'm going to kill you!' I yelled as I tackled him.

My father came rushing into my brother's room and pulled us apart.

He then dragged us to the storage closet outside and said, "Stand right there and shut up," as he rummaged through his self-labeled College Sports Box.

He's not in college, he doesn't play sports, it's just a plain old box, I reflected, as I watched him throw aside basketballs, baseball gloves, and at last come up with what he was looking for ... boxing gloves ... two sets.

Where does he get this stuff? I wondered. I imagined him trolling junk stores, frequenting garage sales or sneaking out for "Moonlight Madness" events. How else to explain the velvet portrait of the Hopi woman with her nursing baby titled "Madonna and Papoose" that he had recently brought home. My father was not religious, he was not Hopi, and he was not—it was evident—a man with a discerning eye for art. Clearly, there was so much we didn't know about how and where he spent his days.

I stood there recalling how my brother, sister, and I just last week had decided to hide in a drained irrigation canal and throw rocks at passing cars. We sat tossing pebbles and mostly missing the cars. All we could see, hidden as we were in the tall grass of the empty ditch, were the tires. The rocks we gathered continued to get bigger, as we hoped for a direct hit and the satisfying sound of contact that would follow. With a couple of good size nuggets we finally scored, hearing the clink and rattle of the rocks on the hubcaps of the unfortunate passerby. We were overjoyed and celebrating our triumph, as if we were bombardiers who leveled the enemy, until we heard a screech of brakes. We saw the tires of our target vehicle on the road above us, backing up, stopping, and then we heard a door open and close, followed by the heavy scrunching of shoes on gravel approaching the edge of the canal and our hiding place. We fearfully waited for the annoyed driver to discover us; we were too scared to run. Before we could even blink twice, we were eye-to-sole with black shoes ... like my father wore. We slowly continued our wide-eyed periscoping up the length of a man's pants, up now to a sport coat ... like my father wore, our eyes now moving in slow motion as we saw something else exactly like his.

His face.

Of all the cars, in all the ditches, in all the world, how could we have hit our father? At this time of day? On this road?

But we did.

I don't know who was more surprised. He expected to confront some juvenile delinquent, we didn't expect to confront anyone. Amidst the yelling about what kind of "nincompoops" throw rocks at cars and what kind of "non compos mentis" sit in canals that the city could flood at anytime, was the sudden realization we were all—and I mean all of us—somewhere we shouldn't be. We looked at him, he looked back at us, and we came to an uneasy, unspoken truce. He told us to walk home and not tell our mother what had just happened, "It would upset her to have more confirmation that her children were so stupid," he said.

"He's not fooling me, he just doesn't want mother to know

he was out on a drive when he should be at work," I tell my brother and sister, who nod their heads in agreement as we dawdle home.

My rock throwing recollection is interrupted by my father saying, "Put these on," while throwing me one pair of boxing gloves, my brother the other.

"Since you both enjoy fighting so much, I want you to go out to the backyard and beat each other up," he continued.

My brother and I blinked rapidly and nervously, turning toward each other, then back to our father.

"I'm not going out to the yard to fight," I said, rolling my eyes, "I'm a lover, not a fighter," I snickered and gave my brother a little push. "But if you insist, can we please call this Outdoor Fun, I think that way I can get a badge for it." I'm cracking myself up and throw a right jab in the air.

"I'll go." My brother was already wearing the gloves and began doing the Teaberry gum shuffle he'd seen on a TV ad.

"You better get those gloves on before the bell, Wisen-heimer," my father warned me as he headed toward the backyard.

"Oh for Pete's sake," I followed him and was about to say something about how I was wearing a dress and couldn't we just once do something mundane, like getting sent to our rooms, when he yelled, "Ding! Round One," and a glove went flying past my left ear. My brother was bringing the heat.

He chased me in circles around the backyard, flailing and swinging and yelling a battle cry that was either "Geronimo" or "Here you go." I managed to get my right glove on, turned his way as he ran past and socked him in the nose, hard. He keened and I cried out "Pow!" and my father yelled, "Ding! Bout over," as he raised my right hand in the air. The whole bout was over in less than forty-five seconds.

"Think about this next time you want to fight. If you say you're going to kill someone, understand what you are saying and how dangerous words can be," he announced.

"Good fight, champ," he smiled at me.

For once, I thought my father was right when he said words can be dangerous. To my brother, a bloody nose was nothing compared to the humiliation involved in hearing the word "champ" applied to me instead of him.

"Better luck next time, chump," he said to my brother.

Back here in the kitchen looking at my destroyed cookies, hating my brother, I feel so, so mad ... but I also sort of get why he would do such a thing. And why he thinks he wants to get back at me ...

My father's nickname for my brother was "pinhead" and he ridiculed him constantly. "Those are your legs?" he teased when my brother wore shorts, "looks more like dental floss coming out of your underwear."

My father made my brother try out for the local NFL punt, pass, and kick football competition. He could neither punt, pass, nor kick, and certainly no one in our house was teaching him how. Nonetheless, my father dragged my brother, against his will, to participate in "a man's sport." I know because he made me come along to watch the impending calamity.

All his schoolmates were at the event, boys who were bigger and stronger and boys who were being cheered on by the dads who had practiced with them. Those boys doubled over laughing when they saw my brother's wobbling throws and missed kicks. My father and I were in the car, watching from the parking lot. When my brother began walking back to the car, his body looked exactly like the Scarecrow from the *Wizard of Oz*, like he had no skeleton. My father deliberately, and making sure my brother could see, locked all the car doors and then wouldn't let him get in the backseat for at least five minutes.

No one said a word on the ride home.

Once I saw my father standing in the hall with my brother bragging about his prowess on the basketball court. My brother was really interested and listening, clearly enthralled by the stories. He looked reverently up at Him and radiated from the glow of my father's shared self-beatification.

I watched wordlessly from the other end of the hall, and I prayed against odds that maybe I was witnessing a rare, warm moment between them. Then I heard my father say,

"When I was your age, I had a letterman's jacket. I think I still have it somewhere," he continued, as he opened the hall closet and began rifling through it looking for the holy shroud he wore in high school. "Ha! Here it is! I knew I saved it." And with that he pulled out his jacket of many colors, covered with golden pins and patches in the shape of basketballs. His name was emblazoned in maroon script down one sleeve, and "1953" knitted in gold thread ran down the other.

Queasiness overtook me as I couldn't help but admit a resemblance between the jacket and my Girl Scout uniform, but my brother actually gasped in reverence when he saw it. It was extraordinary, alright, and I think he must have thought my father was going to give the jacket to him.

My father spun my brother around and said, "Here try this on."

My brother, with his back to my father, happily put his arms in the sleeves—first his right, then the left—and pulled the lapels forward to adjust the jacket before spinning around to glance up at my father for approval.

My father broke into a smile. I held my breath, hoping beyond hope that the space between them could be forever closed by this hand-me-down.

My father picked up the unfilled shoulders of the jacket, which hung loosely on my brother's bony frame, and laughed as he said, "This fit me to a T when I was your age! I was wearing it when I met your mother. A girl would never know you were in there."

He kept laughing as he removed the jacket, hung it back in the closet, and walked away.

I could see on my brother's face that poison mixture of sadness and anger that you see on the faces of the kids being bullied at school. His was the face of a kid who would spend the rest of his life trying to get back at the world— when what he really wanted was to get back at his father.

"So, this is it," I think when I re-focused on my brother's face, next to mine in the cookie caper courtroom, certain of his guilt, "this is the one he has waited for his entire, second-born life." He takes "revenge is sweet" to its highest level. If I wasn't so angry, I might give a handshake to the boy who has bested me.

We are declared guilty on all counts. I'm forced to relinquish my allowance, as are my brother and sister, for close to three months to cover the cost of the cookies. My mother uses them to make pie crusts, we crumble them on top of ice cream, we lay them out as treats whenever anyone drops by, and they still seem to linger. At one point, having these boxes of extra cookies in the house actually saves our lives.

One afternoon my sister and I are watching our favorite cartoon show, *Wallace and Ladmo*, when suddenly my brother comes rushing through the front door, flies past us, runs straight into the bathroom, slams the door, and locks it.

"Must need to go pretty bad," I giggle to my sister as I shut the front door. I no more sit down on the couch to resume watching TV before the front door crashes open again and the worst sight any of the neighborhood kids can ever possibly see walks into our house. It is Donnie Morris.

Now Donnie Morris is the local Boo Radley, minus the kindness and compassion. He is huge, fat, lumbering, and mean. Even if you can't see him you can tell he is nearby because you can smell him. He always smells like rotten eggs.

"Where's the piss ant?" scowls Donnie as he surveys the living room. My sister wets her pants instantly.

"What do you want, Donnie Morris?" I say as I walk toward him holding my nose.

"I want your little brother," he pushes past me tossing aside our chair cushions and magazines. He looks like one of those bears on the *Wonderful World of Disney* who look for food in the trash cans at national parks.

"He's not here," I lie. My brother and I have our differences, but dying at the hands of Donnie Morris is a doom too sorry—and smelly—even for him.

"Well, go find him, gawd dammit."

Why do the big, dumb guys always swear? Do they look in the crystal ball and see what life has in store for them and just give up on vocabulary and hygiene?

"Donnie," I plead, "come on, if I knew where my brother was, I'd hand him over, I promise you."

"I ain't leaving empty handed," he roars.

I stand looking at Donnie, wondering what my next move will be, when I see my wet and droopy panted sister go to the kitchen. I hope she's getting a knife, I think. She comes back with a box of Girl Scout cookies, walks up to Donnie Morris, thrusts the cookies into his grubby and stubby hands and says quietly, "Now you have something in your hands. Good-bye."

It is the bravest thing I have ever seen anyone do. And even though it is only the Shortbread cookies, it works. Donnie Morris looks at that box, then looks at my sister and me, turns, and goes out the door.

The injustice of the cookie sentencing seems to jinx me as a sales person. I discover I don't like to ask people to buy something, it seems like asking them for a favor, and I don't like that either. Never one to give up, I try selling different products in different ways, but each is a disaster that merely confirms my distaste for sales of any kind.

I create a babysitting service, print fliers and hand them out door-to-door in the neighborhood. I ask my sister to come along, hold the fliers and just stand there looking like a small kid I am taking care of—sort of like a testimonial with no testimony—while I sell the neighbors on hiring my "company." My venture is generally well received and I begin to think I might be a sales force after all ... until I get to the house of a friend of mine. I didn't know she lives there. Her mother opens the door and I'm just starting my sales pitch when my friend appears beside her mother and it throws me off.

"Oh, Jeanine, hi! You live here huh?" I stammer. "Uh, oops, I forgot something, I will be right back. Wait right here." At that I bolt from the porch, run down the street and back home, leaving my sister standing at their doorway, literally holding the bag ... of fliers. I don't know how long my sister stands there or what is said, and she never tells me.

I never get hired, either.

The Cookie Connection may deplete my enthusiasm for selling, but all is not lost as it does spur me on to explore other entrepreneurial endeavors.

I become a rabid collector of Bazooka Joe Bubble Gum comics. And I collect thousands of them.

On each playground, at each school I can walk to, there are always hundreds of bubble gum wrappers, with the comics inside, thrown on the ground, ripe for the picking.

It's not that I am an environmental pioneer.

I know that Bazooka Joe comics are redeemable for prizes. Rings, de-coders, whistles, compasses, even books and those cool, colored cardboard pictures you can flick back and forth to make a horse run, or a bird fly. It's miniature magic.

I clear the various playgrounds of the bubble gum wrappers, all year long, then mail in the comics for prize redemption. I became the owner of a huge inventory of prizes. But that is just the beginning.

I catalogue these prizes and then I trade or I barter for better stuff. I even use them as birthday or Christmas gifts for my family and friends.

I also get carried away collecting S&H Green stamps and cereal box tops. I'm like a manic squirrel, collecting them, stashing them, and finally, when the time is right, feeding off of them.

The comic, stamp, box top business I built is how I earn the money to go to Girl Scout Camp in Payson, Arizona for a week.

My pride and excitement in my self-funded adventure is short lived, and all my resourcefulness seemingly ill-spent, when on the first day of camp I'm told that I'm listed first on the latrine cleaning duty list.

I quickly sell my bunkmate on the idea of taking my turn cleaning the vile place in exchange for my Yardley lip gloss, which I acquired by sending in proofs of purchase from Cheerios. In fact, I've wisely stashed a number of my "redeemable with comic or coupon" trinkets in my luggage, which turn out to come in very handy in fending off my many assigned, and onerous, camp tasks. Kitchen duty? Traded to Linda Kopchek for a plastic harmonica and a flower shaped pink barrette. Build the nightly campfire? Done by Gail Perry for a small coin purse with a galloping horse printed on the front. Laundry duty almost breaks my bank, as it's a half-day job that nobody wants. I have to trade one plastic bracelet, two bookmarks inscribed with The Lord's Prayer, and some colored pencils to Taffy, a fellow camper I don't know all that well, but well enough to work the deal.

I go to camp with my fellow scout Sandra Hinkley. Her parents have paid in full for her to go and for some reason her name never appears on latrine duty. She also has her own horse. Her family actually goes somewhere besides the park pool during spring break and her change purse always has money in it. Kids follow her, like those little fish that follow whales, hoping she will share two pennies for a cinnamon sucker at Jose's Corner Market. If you hang around her long enough to become a friend, you get treated to fourteen-cent-french-fries at Burger Chef after school.

Her big house comes complete with something called "the help," people who do laundry, dust furniture, clean their toilets, and even make sandwiches for her whenever she wants one. "The help" have nice quarters with a deck of their own in the back of her house. And they get all of this for doing the chores I have to do every weekend in exchange for a small room I always share with my sister, and if money is tight, with my brother, too.

Soon after Sandra Hinkley comes into my life, my mother gets her first job as a receptionist on Saturdays at Venus DeMilo Beauty Spa. She never even tells us she is looking for a job, or that she gets a job, or will be gone for her job every Saturday. With no warning, one Saturday we are jolted out of bed to the blasts of my father playing "Reveille" on the trumpet he played in high school.

"Today we clean this house from top to bottom," he proclaims as he hands us each our "kits." Mine has a dish towel and butter knife, along with Pledge furniture polish in it.

"Where's mother?" my sister groggily asks.

"Mother has a job on Saturdays, and to celebrate, we are going to clean this place up. Every square inch."

This routine goes on Saturday after Saturday for months. We use toothbrushes to clean the grout, take out light bulbs to dust them, and employ toothpicks to scrape out the gunk around the kitchen sink. And the butter knife? We cover it with a dishcloth to clean between the slats on the venetian blinds and wipe along the baseboards. My father is fastidious in his supervision of us doing the dirty work. We never break for lunch, we clean from morning until early evening when, at last, he takes us to get a hamburger and shake, then sends us to our room and tells us to stay there so he and mother can have a quiet dinner.

Every Saturday night following a day spent with Mr. Clean we are exhausted and look like something removed from the oven too soon ... not quite formed and collapsing in the middle.

Familiarity, I find, breeds "attempt" as I spend most of the evenings confined in our room coming up with half-baked ideas to overthrow our dictator. It is while swilling my watery milkshake one night that I tell my siblings how grand the servants at Sandra Hinkley's live.

"They get their own deck! They can have their own pet!"

We look around at our antiseptic, concrete-block walled bunker and I urge them to consider the benefits of working, and living, with Sandra.

Perhaps, I laugh with them, the missing ingredient in having the three of us get along and be happy is another move ... to someone else's house! Ha-ha.

My sister tattletales to my father the stories I share about moving to Sandra Hinkley's, so I am forbidden to play with her anymore.

I miss my friend and long for another family where siblings didn't squeal or steal from you. And your parents want to have dinner with you.

❧

"The golden pin for Most Cookies Sold goes to ..."

Ronda Beaman.

Turns out I don't have to say who bought all sixty cases, just that I have the receipt for selling them. I have the receipt alright, and it bears my sister's and brother's name—alongside mine on the bottom line.

My troop leader tells me she is quite impressed that I have such supportive siblings.

"The Cookie Connection Badge is awarded to ..."

Ronda Beaman.

Thanks to my brother's spiteful search and destroy act, along with advances on our allowances, I am celebrated as a Girl Scout sales leader.

But, if I'm really any good as a salesperson, or a smart enough cookie, I'd sell my brother on the fact that it isn't me, but the man who once wore a letterman's jacket who is the real crumb.

Learning to get along with people is a skill you will value
throughout your life.

GIRL SCOUT BADGE BOOK

Healthy Relationships

I am swimming at the high school pool. It's August in Phoenix, which means 110 degrees in the shade, so everyone and their mother within ten miles of the place is camped out and trying to cool off here. Including my Girl Scout troop. It is crowded, noisy, and smells like Clorox and coconut oil. I have "Summer Blonde" sprayed in my hair, hoping to get more golden highlights than chlorine green streaks before seventh grade begins.

I am feeling especially "cool" because my mother bought me the cute swimsuit I am wearing at a garage sale last weekend. It is a generous two-piece, showing just a touch of midriff and sports a flouncy skirt in denim with red plaid trim that almost looks like a cheerleader skirt. I am already five feet three inches tall and think there may be a future for me as a Pan Am stewardess.

I am splashing and playing tag with my Coppertoned, but still sunburned and waterlogged Girl Scout friends. I am in the shallow end, standing in about four feet of water when out of nowhere, and from behind, I am grabbed. I think it is part of the tag game I've been playing, so I laugh and flip back off my feet expecting to see a girl behind me. I look up and see the faces of two older boys. I gasp but get no air as they push me under.

I see four legs surround me as I'm kicking and flailing, desperately trying to free myself and come up for air. They are playing too rough and I will tell them so when I re-surface. The boy who seized me now holds the top of my head with one hand and pushes me underwater until I am flattened against the bottom of the pool. He uses his free hand to grope my chest, grabbing both rapidly and harshly under the frilly plaid top of my sweet, new bathing suit. I see another boy swimming underwater toward me, his face is close to mine and I squeeze my eyes shut as he thrusts his hand down the bottoms of my bathing suit and rubs roughly between my legs. It finally dawns on me that this is not a game.

The whole episode lasts less than fifteen seconds, then as suddenly as they appeared, they disappear, swimming back into the chaos and throng of a public swimming hole on a scorching day.

I stand—for what seems like the rest of the afternoon, but is only a couple of minutes—before I walk backward through the shallow end and toward the pool steps, all the while watching the dog paddlers, the splash wars, and the young Mother's bouncing their babies in the ripples. I see a friend wave to me as she jumps off the diving board. My other friends yell to her, "Cannonball!"

I wave back.

The girl in the garage sale bathing suit, with the flouncy skirt, climbing out of the pool is not the same girl who jumped in. Up until now, all the forces against me seemed surmountable and domesticated, mere childhood nuisances. Until today I was guided by the tenets of scouting and powerfully purposed in my pursuits. I was indefatigable and buoyed by optimism. Now, at this moment, I feel a peculiar and unfamiliar combination of losing and being robbed, yet feeling like I'm somehow responsible for what I've lost. I feel, for the first time, there might be something wrong with me, something unsuitable with being an *F* for female.

I watch one of my wet footprints dry before taking another step, I watch the next print dry, and then the next as I plod, one foot lingering in front of the other, on the blazing sidewalk that leads into the locker room.

I change into my shorts and cotton top, pull on my Keds and throw my fancy cheerleader-like suit into the trashcan as I walk out the door and head home.

I decide not to tell anyone. Mostly because I have no one to tell.

In the bright light of day, and still wet behind the ears, I examine where I really stand in terms of my relationships. Earning more badges than anyone in my troop, winning every spelling bee in school, insisting that I be pitcher if I play baseball, dominating the playground tetherball, and moving to different houses in different neighborhoods every three months or so does not tend to create warm and supportive friendships. Being the big, bossy sister isn't cuddly. And if my father thinks I would steal my own cookies, what would he think I did to cause this attack, if I could somehow even find the words to explain it?

Nope, I have no one to tell.

So, walking home I come to a decision not to think about what happened at the pool. I will not remember the four legs circling me underwater and penning me in like prison bars. I will not allow myself to recall the panic and suffocation ever again. I will block this day from my mind. I will remain clean in thought, word, and deed.

I decide that when my mother asks me, I will say I left my new bathing suit in the locker room. I will say I am sorry and I decide I will take the punishment, in whatever form it may come.

Four days from now school is starting and I throw my energies into the frenzy of preparation. What will I wear? What color notebook to buy?

I lose the guilty feeling that has been plaguing me since my troop outing to the pool. I am enthused about a fresh start and vow that I will cooperate rather than compete with others.

I swear there will be no more episodes like the 600-yard-run disaster in my life ...

All of the seventh grade girls had to run in the event, but in reality it was me against my friend and troop buddy, as well as my stiffest competition, Sandra Tognoni. Whoever came in first place also won the coveted spot as captain of the track team.

The race started out well enough. We wished each other good luck, stood side-by-side as the whistle was blown and then BAM! I took the lead. I was running like the wind and smelled of orange groves. I had read about an Olympic runner who puts an orange slice under his tongue to stay hydrated, so I decided what's good enough for the

Olympics is good enough for me and shoved an orange segment in my mouth, too.

Sandra Tognoni was at least three lengths behind me as I cleared the half-way mark. We were not running on a track, we were running the circumference of the school, through the parking lot, around the main building, and back into the baseball fields. The terrain was far from smooth, so watching my footing was a necessity. As I pulled into the final stretch of the race, Tognoni close behind, I lost my ability to breathe. Maybe it was the orange slice blocking my windpipe, maybe I had not paced myself correctly, or maybe Sandra Tognoni was simply a better runner than I. I could see her from the corner of my eye getting close to passing me, I heard the loud cheering from the track coach, PE teachers, and all the boys from seventh grade waiting for their turn to race. We were neck and neck, but I could tell I had nothing left and would lose.

Did I dig deep and muster my innermost resources? Did I smile as my friend Sandra won fair and square and congratulate her as she rightfully took her first prize win? Did I accept that being second place was good enough?

I fell.

Accidentally ... on purpose.

I buckled my knees, and fell dramatically as if I hit a hole in the ground. I lay there in writhing fake pain as Sandra passed me to win the race.

The coaching staff, teachers, and a number of boys came over to help carry me off the field. Everyone was so busy helping me that no one congratulated Sandra at the finish line. I was hand carried to the school nurse, who then drove me to a doctor's office. They called my parents to tell them where they could come pick me up. After taking an

X-ray of my so-called hurt knee my parents arrived concerned, but mostly relieved that no one had tried to contact the family doctor whose name my father had forged. The school doctor pronounced my fake injured-to-preserve-my-dignity knee was sprained, which I guess is why people say doctor's "practice medicine."

I didn't have to do dishes for a week and I got to stay home from school for two days. While home, the door bell rang one afternoon and I limped across the living room to open it only to find Sandra Tognoni holding a plate of get well cookies she made for me. She added the final barb to any shred of dignity I had at this point by telling me that she had suggested to the coaches that we be co-captains of the team.

What a schmuck I am, I think, as I nibble on the cookies. I cheated Sandra, and she brings me a treat. I appall myself. What kind of girl does things like this?

OK, I guess I do. But not anymore. I consider the pool assault to be a warning to develop some healthy relationships. And I need to do so quickly. It's not just the badge I want, it's the companionship and my self-respect.

The night before school starts, as usual, I cannot sleep. I lay awake thinking about everything else with the exception of what happened at the pool. I stare into the dark, picturing myself in the red skirt and pink blouse I have selected for my debut as a seventh grader. It's daring, pink and red, I think, but not outcast daring.

My review of the pressing issues in my life is interrupted by some light clinking sounds.

I sit up, turning my right ear toward my bedroom door and stop breathing as I listen.

Yes, definitely clinking ... like wind chimes but not as many clinks. Followed by some muffled laughter.

I get up, wide awake, and tiptoe to my bedroom door, open it quietly and slink down the dark hallway. I hear more giggling and some really cheesy, slow piano music coming from the living room. The shuttered doors—the very same doors I had cleaned slat-by-slat a few days before—leading from the hallway to the living room are closed. A dim, flickering, almost candlelight-ish hue shines through them.

I approach the shut shutter and peer through the slats. Glancing to my left on the coffee table is a bucket. It is the plastic bucket we usually use on Saturdays when we wash windows. Oh yes, I know that bucket very well.

Are my parents actually cleaning the house without us? At this hour? I stupidly wonder.

Upon looking through a different angle of slat, bending my head so far to the right that my ear is practically resting on my shoulder, I can see, what? It looks like a bottle standing in the middle of the bucket. Arching my head and stretching, this time to the left, with one eye squinting, I can make out two wine glasses on the coffee table alongside two smoldering cigarettes in an ashtray.

"Turn around," my father says, startling me and I jump back when I hear him.

Is he talking to me? My heart is now pounding so loud, I am sure it will give me away. I freeze in place, one eye looking through the slats, still crouched and twisted hoping to get a good view.

"I said, turn around baby, slowly."

OK, whew, not me, he doesn't call me baby. And what's with his tone of voice? It's thick and syrupy, like he's sucking on a Luden's cherry cough drop or something.

I look, with not a small amount of the "oh-oh" feeling in my stomach and a sharp pain in my twisted torso, which is now bearing to the extreme lower right, and see a nearly naked woman I call mother in a pair of flimsy and stringy underwear that don't cover much.

That has to be uncomfortable and cold, I shudder.

The shuddering is premature. My peeping continues higher up her body and the reward for completing the acrobatic task is the sight of some paraphernalia attached to her nipples. There are two gold, glittery cones jutting out a good four inches from her breasts. They are suspended in mid-air, defying gravity and maiming any innocence about what I have to look forward to as an adult.

The back of my mouth starts to water like before I vomit.

My mother begins prancing back and forth in the glitter get-up and I sink to the ground and am eye level with her white high heels.

From the left side of the living room my father issues a moan of sorts. Then he began directing my mother to "Look this way, work it, yeah baby."

Oh dear God, I too, moan and begin to scramble up to beat a hasty retreat but am pulled back in by the sound of a loud clack and "whussh."

What the heck? ... to my utter alarm, I see that he is snapping photos with our Polaroid camera—the same one we use to shoot nice, sweet photos of birthday cakes, Easter egg hunts, and other chaste family events. My mother is laughing, posing, and tossing the small pillows from the couch at him, running her fingers through her red hair, and pouting her even redder lips.

By this point I'm woozy and wobbly. Once again, I back slowly away from a scene I DO NOT want to remember. Even in our ninety degrees house I feel a cold shiver down my spine as I tumble and plop back into my twin bed. My legs are rubbery, my stomach is aching, and I now need a glass of water to keep me from gagging. But there is no way I'm going back out there to fetch one for fear of what I will see next—it might strike me blind!

I lie in the dark of my room, next to my naive and unsophisticated sister, and I know two things for sure. First, I will never tell anyone what I saw. Again, whom will I tell? My sister? No. My teacher? I don't know who my teacher is yet. Troop leader? Uh, no ... who knows what badge, or counseling, that might garner. Silence is the way to go.

Second, I will never, ever get married, not even to a prince or a Beatle.

OK, three things. I will also never wear those things on my nipples.

I finally fall asleep—or faint, I am not sure which. Luckily there are no visions of anything dancing through my head.

The next morning, my mother wakes me up when she opens our bedroom door and tells me to get dressed, "I need to cut your bangs before you leave for school."

I was born with big, blue eyes, a wide grin, and a very high forehead. Two out of three ain't bad. Even as a newborn I looked like I had a receding hairline. I go to great lengths to keep the upper levels of my cranium covered by my bangs. After I shampoo, and before I set my hair in big plastic curlers, I use yards of hair tape to plaster my bangs flat against my formidable brow. Hair tape is pulled off of a rolling dispenser, like regular scotch tape, but it looks more like fabric and does not tear my hair out when I yank it off. With my hair curled, my taped bangs straight, and lots of Aqua Net hair spray, I can almost prevent my hair from moving and thus exposing what on me should be called a five-head.

As a double precaution, I always keep my head down on windy days. I miss a lot of scenery, but that's a price I gladly pay.

When my mother cuts my bangs, she does it for real. She wants the trim to last at least six weeks, which means she massacres my forelocks. When she's finished with me I have to walk around with my eyebrows raised for days on end to make my bangs look longer.

I do not want to spend my first day as a seventh grader with bangs too short, eyebrows disconcertingly raised, and the resulting gigantic headache.

Once dressed, I take my sweet time heading to the kitchen. Seeing my mother holding the scissors and picturing the humiliation of soon-to-be too short bangs, I immediately start to cry. Bawling like a baby in a big body would be more accurate.

"Are you really crying over a haircut? At your age?" my mother sighs, clearly finding my dramatics irksome.

I sit down and she wraps a towel around my shoulders and begins to cut.

She has pushed me too far by pulling out the "big girls don't cry" card and I am forced to defend myself.

What my mother doesn't know, while wielding those scissors and making fun of my tears, is what blackmail material I now possess and how low I will go to keep my bangs long. This is self-image-defense. I am convinced that once she knows I know how she spends her evenings, the scissors will drop, she will run to her room and hide, and I can keep my tresses unscathed as I march merrily to school.

I retort with a gulp, sniffle, and choke, "I am not crying about my hair ... I am crying because ... I am crying because ... of what I saw last night ... when I got up to go to the bathroom."

As according to my plan, the scissors stop in mid-cut. There is a palpable intake of air as she holds them aloft and whispers feebly, "What do you mean ... what exactly did you see?"

"You and Daddy" ... I like the way this is going and delay my response for an instant to build up the suspense ..., "dressed in funny stuff and taking pictures."

She quits whittling away at my bangs and stands perfectly still as I regal her with the minute and freakish details of what I had witnessed. The more of the sordid event I recall, the more zombie like she becomes. Moving very slowly she hands me an empty lunch pail and sends me to school with only half the bang butchering done.

I am left with the challenge of half long, half short bangs. This predicament requires mastery of the one-arched-eyebrow-one-eye-half-shut look, just to even everything out. I spend my first day at school looking like Popeye.

At the end of the day my face is semi-paralyzed, so when no one can see me I stretch my face back out and begin the walk home. I have been too distracted by the changing classrooms and different teachers for each subject that come with junior high to give any further thought to what had happened at home that morning.

My mind is proving to be quite gymnastic in its capabilities to deny, disavow, and make certain events in my past completely disappear.

I only think of the Polaroid party when I see my father behind the wheel of his gold dust colored Monterey, waiting at the curb. When he sees me, he opens his door and steps out of the car. He is wearing his usual business suit, dark glasses, and smoking a cigarette. It looks like the FBI has come for me.

I sort of wish it was the FBI. I would have plenty of things I could tell them and a kindly agent might bring me a doughnut after the questioning. However, with my father I feel pretty sure I will be lucky if he gives me a ride all the way home and doesn't drop me off in the desert like our errant dog.

"Mother tells me you saw something," he starts the conversation as I hop in and we pull away from the school grounds.

Oh geez, I think as I draw my top lip down and knit my eyebrows to relieve the lingering frozen face pain from the day.

"Yes," I manage, through stretched lips.

"Do you want to talk about it?" he presses.

"No." I am picturing him in his underwear holding the camera and I'm perhaps permanently mute.

"Are you sure? It might do you some good to talk about it." He has moved into an inauthentic, sympathetic tone. It is the kind of offer school officials warn you about when a man pulls up in a car and wants to give you candy.

I'd rather shave my head, I silently scream.

"No, really, no," I reply through my tightening lips.

"Maybe you would rather talk with mother?"

Or how about NO ONE! I yell in my sore head.

"Yes," I gurgle as I shrink down in my seat.

So, thankfully, he does drive me straight home.

Later that night, I get to stay up after the rest of the family goes to bed. I know something is up when mother says I can watch Johnny Carson with her, even though it is a school night.

We don't even hear his monologue, in fact Skitch Henderson has barely finished leading the orchestra in the *Tonight Show* theme before she says,

"Do you have any questions?"

My parents are not big on the warm up.

"No," I groan.

"Do you know what you saw?" she smiles but looks straight ahead at the Magnavox.

I have permanently blocked it from my high forehead, I think.

"Yes," I say.

While staring at the television, she then begins some disjointed tales of her dating life that result in this moral, "Many times when you go out with boys you have to walk home, but married people share one body. In fact a boy named Terry drove me all the way to Long Beach and when I said no, he left me there."

Huh? I am trying to follow her, truly I am, but I am having a tough time connecting the dots from white high heels-to-Polaroids-to-Terry-and-then-back-again-to-Johnny Carson and walking home if you tell a boy "no."

The best I can figure out from the whole incident is this—if I don't date I will always have a ride home and if I never get married I don't have to divide myself in half or wear silly underwear.

And I don't want a Polaroid camera in my house.

My relationships are far from healthy and bordering on anemic, like many of my accomplishments. I am learning that my bonds with others have been shallow, founded on silences, secrets, and my own stupidity.

I am not relating with others even at my cherished and highly anticipated Girl Scout events.

A month or so following the strip show, at our first sleep-over of the year, my troop leader is talking about the Healthy Relationships badge. We are huddled around her sipping on the Fizzies we have made and having the kind of cozy *Little Women* evening I relish and only find in scout gatherings. And then, she ruins it by saying, "Marriage is the most important relationship of all."

I cringe and lie all the way down and stare at what I call the "Las Vegas"ceiling that is so popular in the southwest. It's the kind with little shiny, sparkly flakes mixed into the bumpy paint, as if shimmering makes the ceiling something more than a ceiling.

"And girls," she says, as the rest of them hang onto every word, their little heads sticking out of the cheap sleep sacks festooned with images of Barbie, Unicorns, or Cinderella, "my husband told me that if I hadn't been a virgin, with a capital V, he would have dropped me like a hot potato."

What? A what? I am mulling this statement over in my mind, but the others girls seem to be taking the remark in stride.

I pop up on my elbows asking, "What is a virgin?"

Now usually I like all eyes on me, but not tonight, not like this. Everyone is looking at me with the fourth-grade teacher pity-puss I am unfortunately all too familiar with. "What?" I say incredulously ... "I suppose you all know," I say to them in a nah-nah-nah-nah-nah type rhythm.

The troop leader smiles sympathetically and says, "If you don't know, Ronda, then you should ask your mother. It's not up to me to tell you about such things."

I lie back down and see the troop leader shaking her head and rolling her eyes at the other girls, who all seem to be united in their sympathy toward my backwoods Elly May Clampett ways.

Brother, I think, so far growing up stinks. There are simply too many mysteries and too many previously fun things that are all of a sudden perilous. Like swimming in the same pool with boys. Or having a troop sleepover turn into marriage counseling. I fall asleep afraid I am outgrowing scouts or, worse, I am getting left behind.

To top it all off, school is suddenly problematic.

It's not that I get into big trouble at school. I like school too much, I am comforted by the consistency of a classroom, and I feed off the positive feedback I get from most of my teachers. It's just moving around so much leaves me unable to connect with a role model, a mentor, or a good friend. I enjoy meeting new people, I am a chatterbox, and I like being in front of a crowd, I just can't get much deeper than that.

Sometimes, I get caught talking in class when I shouldn't and I'm asked to be quiet. Once in awhile I get carried away and I keep talking out of turn, like I do one day in Mr. Clark's class.

Mr. Clark is the first male teacher I have, other than my father. I don't know what to expect and, truthfully, I'm a little frightened. Mr. Clark has a thick thatch of brown hair, he wears wire rimmed glasses and in many ways resembles President Theodore Roosevelt. He knows this and has dubbed his homeroom students "The Roughriders." He is impeccably dressed most days in a crisp, white, short-sleeved shirt, a red tie, and light brown slacks with a clean crease that runs the length of both his pant legs.

One day he shows up for class wearing a wrinkled shirt, no tie, stained pants, and wild hair that goes in every direction but down. He has also forgotten his glasses. He is quite a sight. The whispers from the students begin almost immediately as we make fun of him and create infantile jokes to explain his attire, "His wife must have kicked him out for impersonating a President" and "Looks like he had a rough ride himself." All of us snicker and giggle and think we are so hilarious and clever. He continues to be the major source of amusement at recess and in the cafeteria. "What happened to his hair? He looks like he stuck his finger in an electric socket." "I wonder what trough he will be having dinner in tonight?"

At the end of the day, during my hour in his class, he finally breaks down and tells his story. His beloved dog died last night. Mr. Clark sat up with his pet all night before they put the dog down which left Mr. Clark without any sleep and no time to shower or change clothes. He knows, he says, that we have all been making fun of how he looks. "But not one of you has come up to ask me if I am alright, or if you can help me. Not one of you tells me to my face that my hair is messed up, you all just laugh at me behind my back, like cowards and bullies. From this day forward, I hope you will remember how poorly you have treated me today and give people the respect and compassion they need and deserve. You can never know what it is like to walk in another man's shoes. I suggest you practice compassion and empathy rather than criticism and name calling."

This might be the most important tutorial I will ever be given in school.

Mr. Clark continues throughout the year to teach me valuable lessons that serve me well, and I consider his instruction for my betterment to be a healthy relationship when I need it most.

One afternoon he finally has enough of my chattering to others instead of paying attention to him.

He asks me to step outside, follows me out the door, tells me to put my nose against the supporting pole between the roof and sidewalk, and says, "Since you like talking so much, talk to this pole. And talk non-stop. Every time I walk by the door, you better have your nose against the pole and be talking to it." With that, he heads back inside to an amused class.

I admire his creative approach and do just as instructed. It happens to be troop meeting day, so I am in full uniform as I address the pole.

"Hello pole, how are you today? Yes, Mr. Pole, it is a lovely day."

Other students or teachers walking by stare, or laugh, or ask me who my skinny friend is, but I do not waiver, nor do I keep quiet. I talk incessantly to the pole, and only the pole.

"Pole, would you like some gum?" I see Mr. Clark heading from the far end of the classroom toward the door to check on me.

"Why yes, pole, I do think Mr. Clark is a fine teacher. I like him very much."

At that Mr. Clark laughs and lets me back in class, thus increasing my healthy relationships total by two—my teacher and a metal pole.

Polling is the extent of my crime and punishment at school until the Jimmy Barrera fiasco when preserving my dignity loses to my wanting to have friends.

Jimmy, a pal only because his name starts with a *B*—but beggars can't be choosers—is passing a paper to me in English class one day and out of left field quietly says,

"You're so dumb, you don't even know where babies come from."

"I do too."

At this Mark Finizza, across the aisle, laughs and joins in, whispering, "You don't know, I am one hundred percent sure you don't know."

The truth is, I have no idea. I have my Betsy Wetsy doll who, although anatomically correct, doesn't give birth. I know Betsey's body better than my own but feel relatively sure I am savvy enough to figure out the answer. After all, I have some basic information and rudimentary experience in these matters ...

❧

In third grade my father had sat me in his lap and explained that someday I would be riding my bike to school and I would bleed between my legs.

"This is normal. When it happens, just go to the school nurse." He said this as though it happens to everyone. It felt forced sitting on his lap and then I felt creepy talking about blood on my underwear. No surprise that I blocked this discussion totally from my mind. So totally that by the seventh grade when I did bleed, I had forgotten all about "the talk."

I was at chorus practice, rehearsing songs for an assembly. I felt ill, and achy, like I was coming down with the flu. When I got home and went to the bathroom, I saw blood on my underwear. I broke down, weeping on the bathroom floor, claiming to whoever was listening, "I'm too young to die."

I took what I was sure was my final shower, fell again to my knees crying about how there was still so much for me to do in life and begged for mercy.

I bravely pulled myself together and dressed for the assembly. *The show must go on,* I said to my reflection in the steamy mirror, channeling Ethel Merman.

When I came out of the bathroom, I thought I should go kiss my mother good-bye ... as in a "Heavens to Murgatroyd, exit stage left" good-bye.

I approached her, she was sitting on the couch reading something in a Reader's Digest Condensed Books, and slowly and solemnly leaned in to kiss her, like Bela Lugosi in those vampire movies.

"What are you doing? You're still wet," she said.

"I have come to say good-bye," I dripped with finality as I soaked up her face.

"It's way too early for the assembly." She looked up at our sunburst black and gold wall clock, the black metal hands on four o'clock. "You're not leaving now, are you?"

Ironically the big number we had been rehearsing was "No Man Is An Island" and as I stood in front of my mother, replaying in my head the lyrics,

> " ... No man stands alone
> Each man's joy is joy to me ... " I was moved to announce,

"Yes, I am leaving. I am dying, I am sick, and I may not make it to the assembly."

I told my mother the awful truth, I confided in her and, like a Southern Belle with the vapors, told her that I didn't want to die this gruesome death without letting her know I loved her.

She grabbed me by the hand, walked me down the hall and told me to lay down on her bed. She pulled the drapes shut and closed her bedroom door.

Is she going to call a doctor? I wondered. Or an ambulance? I was expecting a warm blanket, or maybe some of that bread soaked in milk she gives us when we are sick. I was also hoping for lots of wailing about how empty her life without me would be. Instead, she told me to spread my legs as she reached up for my underwear, pulled them down, and looked into my up-until-now private parts. She once had to insert a pill in my rear end, and I took minor comfort at this moment in knowing she hadn't had time to get either a pill or a thermometer.

"Ronda Ann, you are not dying. This is your period. Congratulations! Today you are a woman."

My prize was a trip to the market for a white lace elastic belt with a hook in the front and a hook in the back, and a three foot high purple box with gigantic lettering that spelled KOTEX. There were even drawings on the inside flap showing me how to use my new womanly accessories. I didn't know all the particulars about why I was bleeding and frankly, there was no solace in knowing that it happens to all women.

Not knowing why we have one, or what a period is for, was only the tip of the iceberg in my anatomy ignorance. I had recently walked behind a Basset Hound with a fellow Girl Scout on a hike and asked what the things dangling between his legs were. She doubled over, laughing, and when she saw I was serious, she tried to muffle her guffaws as she said something that made no sense whatsoever. She simply said, "Balls."

"What are they for?" I continued, to her apparent shock, for once again—as was getting to be a pattern with most of the people I interacted with—she just stared at me.

She picked up her hiking pace and simply said, "Come on."

My point exactly, I think. *Come on, can someone please tell me, what are dog balls for?*

Now, faced with the pressure to answer my critics and prove I know where babies come from, I do what I have always done when I don't know the answer, have the skills, or own the right equipment—I fake it. Between Miss Wetsy, my period, and dog balls, I am bound to come up with some semblance of an appropriate answer to the birthing of babies.

"Quiet over there in the corner," the English teacher Mr. Lewis warns, looking right at me. How come when there is talking going on, teachers automatically think it is the girl, not the boy? In my case it is generally a fair assumption, but this time I resent the implication.

"Go ahead, Smarty Pants, tell us where babies come from," Jimmy taunts under his breath.

"Yeah, this outta be good," Mark chuckles.

And then I do the stupidest thing possible, I tell them.

Or at least I tell them what I'm able to patch together, given the breadth and depth, or more exactly the shallowness, of my knowledge.

"Babies come out of the same hole that you do number two."

This seems plausible since that is the only hole "down there" that, to my knowledge and limited experience, can stretch big enough for a baby to enter the world. Babies have to come into this world like poop.

At this, Jimmy and Mark go into what can fairly be described as convulsions. Loud fits of hysteria that start combustible laughter from the rest of the class. Jimmy falls to the floor and lies on his back kicking his legs in the air like a cockroach. Mark stands ramrod straight on his chair and howls as tears stream down his face.

Hmm ... I must be wrong, I think, replaying my answer in

my mind as Mr. Lewis rushes from across the room to our corner demanding to know what in the world is going on.

"It's Ronda, Mr. Lewis, Ronda told a joke and it's killing us, killing us," Jimmy guffaws.

"Come down from that chair, Mr. Finizza," Mr. Lewis yells.

Oh man, these guys are gonna get it now, I think, because I know Mr. Lewis likes me and besides, what could I ever say that's funny enough to warrant floor rolling? He will, for sure, know it's the boys who started this whole thing.

Miss Beaman, would you like to tell me, in fact, tell the whole class, what funny joke you just told?" Mr. Lewis asks in that fake calm and mannerly way adults do when they are really mad at you.

"I didn't tell a joke, sir, I just answered a question that Jimmy asked," I reply truthfully, as is my new and improved way.

"Fine, Miss Beaman, let's have the question and then the answer that seems to have been so very, very, funny."

Not only do I not want to tell what the question was, because I know my answer is wrong, I don't want to say it again, out loud, and share my ignorance publicly, either.

"Yeah, Ronda, I think you should tell Mr. Lewis what you said," Jimmy laughs.

"I can't, Mr. Lewis. I can't." I now have tears in my eyes, too, but they are from fear and panic.

"Miss Beaman, why are you saying things that cannot be repeated to me? That is unladylike and unbecoming. If you can't say it to everyone, you shouldn't say it at all."

"Yes, sir."

"And I will give you a week in detention to think about what you say and who you say it to, is that clear?" he says as he struts back to his desk.

"But Jimmy and Mark asked the question first, aren't they coming to detention too?" I ask.

"No, Miss Beaman, it was you who chose to answer, it was you who caused the commotion, and it will be you sitting in detention. Is that clear?"

"Clearly unfair," I shot back.

"Pardon me?" Mr. Lewis briskly turns back towards me.

"Yes, sir."

The week in detention gives me time to think about all that is happening to me, to my body, and to my spirit. Much of what I'm experiencing is certainly not fair, but like my father always tells me, "Who ever told you life is fair?"

No one.

For me, the entire seventh grade is an unsuccessful search for a hand I can hold to guide me through the random land mines of the promised unfair life.

My parents are preoccupied holding each others hands, among other body parts. My siblings, too, hold on to each other. My teachers accept my raised hand for classroom monitor or to help organize bulletin boards. But not one teacher ever chooses to talk to me about anything other than schoolwork.

And friends? Sure, at each school, in each district, and with every new state, I make friends, I join activities, I become an evolved extrovert. Yet, I know I will be moving and therefore, cannot afford, emotionally, to hold on to any of them too steadfastly. Although the Girl Scout laws and badges provide a moral compass, as well as ongoing goals and awards, the Healthy Relationships badge only confirms what I think I knew all along.

I lack the deep connection with others that even earning my badge cannot provide. Although I yearn for a relationship with a lifelong friend and I crave a lasting bond with a role model who can bring out my potential, I discover I won't find a hand from my family, teachers, or even troop leaders to pull me out of the deep pool of disappointment and denial in which I'm beginning to sink.

You know more than you think.
And this badge will prove it.
Find creative solutions to everyday problems.

GIRL SCOUT BADGE BOOK

Creative Solutions

I am dressed in my father's sport coat, wearing a top hat I made from an oatmeal cylinder spray painted black, and pounding the pavement with a cane I fashioned from a baseball bat, also painted black with a white tip. "Come one, come all to the See-Worthy Carnival." I announce to the smattering of friends, scouts, and neighbors gathered around me—the master of ceremonies.

By the summer following seventh grade, not thinking about what the boys did to me at the pool, not remembering what happened between my parents that night in our living room, and forgetting about the healthy relationships I lack, gives me an empty enough head to come up with a creative solution to ease my mounting amnesia. I won't be a star, or solve the race to space crisis, or give birth ... but I can create miracles.

I can be Anne Sullivan, the teacher who saved Helen Keller.

Wanting to be Mouseketeer Annette Funicello—with a short stop at dreaming of wearing a crown like Miss America Vonda Kaye Van Dyke, or being the first girl in space—and then deciding to be a miracle worker is a major leap on the personal evolutional scale, I think as I watch the movie scene of Annie teaching Helen what water is and then what she needs to know to sign the word. This movie isn't about Helen, it's about her teacher, that's who the *Miracle Worker* is and that is who I want to be.

Which is how I find myself standing in our driveway, facing the growing throng who have paid five cents a piece to stand in our front lawn for what I named, The See-Worthy Carnival. From inception to production, and every step in-between, I've created this fundraising event for the Indian School for the Blind in downtown Phoenix.

Motivated by both the Creative Solutions badge and Anne Sullivan I turn our driveway into "The Big Top" with the help of a white sheet attached to four ladders. I recruit fellow scouts, talented neighbors, and my brother and sister to help. Even my mother gets excited about the carnival and bakes cupcakes decorated with circus animal crackers on top and offers to work the refreshment stand.

"Before your very eyes, today, and today only, you will witness feats of magic" I yell, and cue Larry. He's an old man down our street who does card tricks and I've recruited him to help by offering to wash his windows. Larry runs, well shuffles, down the driveway from inside my house and takes his place to my right. He is wearing a shiny silver shirt with lime-green shorts and is flipping his deck of cards back and forth in mid-air.

The crowd roars. OK, the crowd moderately claps.

I tap my "cane" on the driveway and continue, "Next, ladies

and gentleman, you will be amazed by the exotic swaying of Maryla the Magnificent."

Maryla Raper, a fellow scout, called me last week and invited me to come to the mall and shoplift make-up. I politely declined. But that invitation is the blackmail material I use to persuade her to dance in a hula skirt with a rose behind her ear. She is wearing plenty of pilfered blue eye shadow and the crowd cheers as she enters and twirls her baton.

"And in the third ring, for your delight and pleasure, ladies and gents ... JUMBO!"

At that cue, my brother blows his trumpet, and four scouts come trampling up hunched inside a gray sheet. The head of my pachyderm has big, pink ears made from pillow cases and a stuffed trunk that once was a wrapping paper tube. With more trumpeting Jumbo twirls in the center of the driveway to the delight and applause of the audience.

The show also includes a boy juggler, some gymnasts doing back bends and cartwheels, a yo-yo demonstration, and a roller-skating Brownie.

After the main show, I have fellow scouts manning a fish pond. For two cents, a patron can get a fishing rod I've made from a metal hanger, cast it into the pond (OK, over the backyard fence) and pull out a little prize ... one of my old toys or a Bazooka comic redemption.

While the carnival crowd mulls around the cupcake and lemonade stand, fishes for prizes, and visits with the performers, I change costumes and become "Madame Olga, the Fortune-Teller."

I'm wearing a black lace nightie of my mothers over my t-shirt and shorts. I have baby powdered my face white and lipsticked my mouth bright red. To cap the ensemble off I wear my mother's multi-flowered, King of Siam swim cap.

I sit in the pitch-black carport storage room, behind a TV tray I have covered with, what else, a sheet, shine a flashlight up at my face and consult not a crystal ball, but a popular toy, the Magic 8-Ball, which serves as my fortune-telling device. For the low, low price of one nickel you get a reading with Madame Olga and this turns out to be a big money maker. There is a line at least ten deep waiting to see Madame Olga and get answers to pressing questions like,

"Will I hit a homerun at the game this week?" or "Does Jeff Myers like me?" when to my abject horror, my mother swings open the door and makes me come out to the carport so she can get some pictures of me with our tainted Polaroid. Once the crowd sees me in the light, the line quickly disperses and Madame Olga is no more.

The See-Worthy Carnival rakes in almost seventeen dollars and a picture of me, with my performers, appears on the front page of the *Arizona Republic*. I have now been featured on the front page twice. Both times I make the news for doing something honest and creative for a good cause. It is clear to me that I'm finally on the right path.

The warm response from the neighborhood and the total support of my Girl Scout troop for the carnival gives me an unfamiliar feeling. I have moved from the self-centered goal of being the best, no matter the cost, to bringing out the best in others, and it makes me feel like I am home.

At long last I am anchored to a place and I have a vision for the future, thanks to the See-Worthy Carnival.

This stability and serenity continues for two whole days.

Then I am blindsided.

"We are moving to Seattle," my father announces as we gather for dinner.

Our meal that night is later than usual. My father has come home early from work, but he and my mother are sitting outside on the patio having a longer than normal cocktail hour. Both are speaking in the hushed voices adults use when discussing what they think are serious things, or when they are doing private stuff while wearing odd underwear. I know they are talking in these tones because, as the oldest child, it is up to me to venture out of our room and gather any intelligence regarding when we might be having food.

I creep into the living room and see the back of their heads through the plastic webbing of the chaise lounges they are sitting in. The ashtrays on both sides of their chairs are full and smoke continues to billow around them. The sky is turning the glorious pink and blue swirl that makes me glad to live in the desert. My parents look like a TV commercial for the good life. They are holding hands, drinking scotch, smoking filtered cigarettes, and staring into the sunset.

I step a little closer, like the good sibling spy that I am, to listen more closely to their murmuring.

"I took the test," or "I need a rest" I hear my father say. Followed by something about sympathy or empathy.

My mother, whose higher pitch is clearer, responds, "How can a written test reveal how sympathetic you are?"

Yeah, you didn't need to take a test, I smirk, you coulda asked me.

Living with my father has made me a master of the "just think it, don't say it" comeback and I think I am getting quite good at silent, but hilarious, repartee.

My father sounds angry, his sentences are short and staccato. I do make out a few words like "idiots," and "morons," words he often uses to describe us, so I perk up, listening extra hard to find out what we have done this time.

I hear my mother say, very clearly and sweetly as she touches his cheek, "You didn't want to be a stockbroker anyway."

At this point I hightail it back to my starving brother and sister with what I think is the complete story.

"He's in a bad mood about some test he took at work. He has no sympathy so he didn't pass, he still thinks we are morons, and he won't be able to break the stocks," I report.

"But when do we eat?" my brother asks as he throws his shoe at my feet.

"It's getting dark, it's almost bedtime," my sister sulks as she falls into herself.

All three of us are pacing in our room, glassy-eyed, like lions at feeding time, when we are eventually called for dinner. My brother and sister roar past me, running full speed toward the dining room.

I, having the confidence of knowing some survival techniques that I've picked up at many Girl Scout field trips—like not running when you are prey—stroll in at my usual pace.

"Stop running in the house," my father yells as they charge to the table.

"That's the first thing you learn. If you run when a bear

approaches, his instinct kicks in and he will chase and kill you," I say with a touch of pride. Not as a comeback, just an interesting fact to contribute that might get me out of doing the dishes tonight.

"What is wrong with you? Sit down."

My father apparently doesn't appreciate my knowledge of life in the wild.

Like every other night, at every dining room in every house we've ever lived in, the seating arrangement was the same. Parents at each end and two sisters on one side—me closest to my father, my sister on my mother's end. And then my brother, all by himself, on the other side.

No matter what time dinner was served, we always passed every bowl of potatoes, beans, applesauce, whatever its contents, to the right. The meat, which might have been round steak that had been hammered and dipped in flour to fry, or maybe canned salmon mixed with egg and saltine crackers to form patties, was already on our plates.

Once a week we had liver because my sister was iron deficient. I was sure I was allergic, but that never got me out of eating my share.

One night I simply couldn't stomach another piece of heinous cow organ and began, bite by bite, to spit it into my linen napkin.

This qualifies as a creative solution I thought as I held my breath before each bite met my mouth. Another survival tactic picked up along the way—if you don't breathe while eating you can't taste the rattlesnake, or in this case the liver. I got dizzy from the lack of oxygen at liver dinners. Spam and beans, as well as all cooked vegetables could also cause me to fall into a code red respiratory failure.

In a house like mine, where children were second-class citizens, having preferences or differences was not encouraged or embraced. I kept trying to explain to my father that I had sensitive taste buds, I couldn't stand things like the pungent taste of broccoli, or limp, overcooked carrots. Not to mention the sheer torture of chewing and swallowing liver.

"Ask mother," I pleaded more than once. "She says I have always been this way."

And more than once my mother would tell the same story; "Ronda was born a finicky eater. Most days she wouldn't even open her mouth. So, I spent hours dancing around the room with a suction dart stuck to my forehead to make her laugh. As soon as she laughed, I'd swoop in and shove a spoonful of peas or a dab of oatmeal into her mouth and start dancing again. By the end of the day I had a big round bruise on my forehead from pulling the dart off and Ronda had enough food in her to make it to the next meal."

I loved this story for multiple reasons. First, the telling of it stalled my eating of … (insert any offending food that brought this topic up—yet again). Second, I liked knowing that my mother was interested in having me live. And lastly, I liked picturing the circular bruise the suction cup left on her head. I suspected that anyone who saw her must have thought my Irish mother was part of a rare Hindu sect.

Regardless of my enjoyment of the story, it never moved my father to excuse me from the table or let me eat a peanut butter sandwich instead of whatever food it was I didn't like.

So, it had come to this ... spitting liver into my napkin and wondering why it had taken me so long to think of doing it.

I was particularly chatty and lively that night, considering there was a large wad of cold liver soaking through the napkin on my lap. Truth is, I was totally pleased with myself, anticipating the moment when I would smugly say, "May I be excused? I need to go to the bathroom," and exit stage left to dump the contents of my napkin in the toilet, where I thought it really belonged.

Following some witty repartee and feeling empowered once the flushing moment arrived, on cue came my request,

"May I please be excused to go to the bathroom?" I said, oh so sweetly, making bold and steady eye contact, with my father.

"Of course," he replied.

HA! I thought as I pushed my chair back from the table, napkin still down in my lap but ready to be folded up and carried off under the plate I planned to clear off the table.

"Good dinner, Mother." I was pushing the envelope now and I acted casual as I began my departure but my adren- alin galloped with the anticipation of victory. I stifled the words I wanted to scream, I will NEVER have to eat liver again! I have solved this problem and as always, the Girl Scouts are right! I *am* smarter than I think I am!

I was now standing, plate in my two hands, napkin clutched under the plate, totally appearing normal, and was turning toward the kitchen when I heard my father say,

"Leave your napkin, Ronda, you will need it for dessert."

Dessert? I panicked. What dessert? Tonight we're having dessert? Tell me this isn't happening. But, remaining as cool as the liver in my napkin, I said,

"Oh, that's OK, I have lots of homework, and I am really full, thanks anyway," and I managed a relaxed chuckle.

"Ronda, please put your napkin on the table." Now he was stern and I knew my plan was cooked.

I must have looked like the liver after my mother boils it, sort of blanched and gray, as I laid my soiled, soaked napkin down where my dinner plate had been.

"Please open your napkin for your brother and sister to see," my father requested, in a monotone Rod Serling on *Twilight Zone* type of way.

I stood at the table, looking down at the napkin as I flipped open the corners, revealing what can only be described as road kill ... or liver.

"EEEWWWW," "Looks like puke," "Oh geeez," and other pithy remarks were shared by my siblings before my father said,

"Ronda, please sit down and finish your dinner."

"What? What do you mean finish my dinner? I can't eat that," I felt cornered, I knew I was going to cry and began pleading, "I would rather kill myself, please don't make me eat this, I won't do it again, I promise, please, Daddy, please don't make me."

"Your mother works hard to cook you good meals and you are going to eat this good meal and then thank your mother for cooking it for you."

"She doesn't make this for me, she makes this for my sister," I argued.

My father stood up so quickly the sheer force knocked his chair over, he came right at me and smacked me across the face.

I staggered backward and fell to the ground. I overdid the collapse for dramatic effect, I think I could have remained standing, but I was hoping his guilt at hitting me so hard would get me out of eating the liver.

"Don't you ever be a smart aleck to me, or criticize your mother again. Do you hear me?" he said as he shook me.

OK, guilt wasn't working.

"Yes."

"Yes what?"

"Yes, sir."

He told me to get up off the floor and sit down at the table, picked his chair back up, excused the rest of the family—who were all pretty quiet by this time—and my father and I sat together at the table, in silence, for almost three hours while he made sure I ate every bite of what I had hidden in my napkin.

While going through the ordeal of the meal, I didn't learn the lesson my father intended for me by forcing me to gnaw the cold, half-chewed liver. I am sure it was something about appreciation, not being deceptive and being grateful. My take-away was something closer to believing my father was a Nazi hiding out in the suburbs of Arizona.

But not a nice Nazi like Colonel Klink on *Hogan's Heroes*. I chewed on this thought and the liver very slowly.

❧

Wait a minute … did he just say we are moving to Seattle? I jerk my head up rousing myself from my semi-conscious-due-to-starvation-state as my stomach falls to the floor.

Before I can confirm what he said, my mother chimes in, "To celebrate our move to Seattle we are having a special, Tribute to the Pacific Northwest, dinner."

Apparently, to mark the occasion, our usual "pass to the right, eat every bite" ritual is being temporarily abandoned.

On our table is a heaping bowl of Ore-Ida french fries and another equally heaping bowl of some roundish white meatballs.

My father, doing a really poor impression of a casual guy, loosens his tie, removes the cufflinks designed to look like the tailgate of a Chevrolet Impala, rolls up the sleeves of his French cuff shirt and says (again impersonating a normal Dad), "Yeah, kids! Dig in."

Take an average t-shirt wearing, beer swilling, watching football, tousling your hair, and playing catch kinda dad, go polar opposite, and there is my father. And, he isn't an especially effective actor, so this abrupt chumminess is alarming and disconcerting. The only thing informal about him is that we all call him "Daddy." About three houses ago, at dinner, my brother asked, "Please pass the butter, Father." My father got up, thumped my brother hard on the back of his head and replied, "Don't ever call me that again, smart ass." So "Daddy" it is when we address him out loud.

I have no appetite for another move and the only thing I

am prepared to dig into is an argument against Seattle, not my dinner.

My ravenous brother and sister pile the potatoes and meat thingys high on their plates. Clearly enjoying this new, laid back chap at the head of our table, as well as the relaxed etiquette, they are wolfing down the food so fast, they don't even react to the announcement about our next move.

I sit frozen in time and space. I am not blinking, but I am thinking.

I am old enough to have an opinion, I am a troop leader, a carnival barker, I give acceptance speeches at Girl Scout banquets ... this is my moment ... say something, say it now. All these thoughts are running through my head as I watch my father put some french fries and a couple of the meatballs on my plate.

"Wait," I blurt. "I don't want to move."

If my brother and sister weren't stuffing their little mouths so full they would probably gasp at my futile foolhardiness.

Then, without warning, my father does a totally unexpected thing.

He bribes me.

When not limited by his galling self-regard, my father can be charming, thoughtful, and even kind ...

I bet even Hitler had a soft spot for his dog.

And my father, every now and then, would be so magnanimous, or show such compassion, or sense of fun that my guard would be let down. Life with him was like having a personal morphine drip. The good news is I got an occasional drop for excruciating pain when I really needed it. The bad news is he controlled the drip. One day he might hold my hand as we walked, and the next day say "How could someone get so ugly in twelve short years?"

In one instant he would be designing a graphic of my name for my school notebook and then not an hour later get angry about the wrong direction I used when I cut the bread in half for his sandwich, " Don't you know how to do anything right?"

He'd drop us off at the curb for Sunday School—with us having eaten no breakfast, so he and mother could have a couple of hours alone—and then pick us up and take us to an amusement park for a fun afternoon of cotton candy and bumper cars.

In fact, my father was like an amusement park—sometimes, but not always, worth the price of admission. Some rides were fun, and some made me sick. And it was impossible to tell if the experience would be any good until it was over.

"Look, Ronda, I know this will be a tough relocation for you. You've done a good job fitting in and making friends every time we move. You will do the same this time, I am sure. But to make it easier, if you don't cry and carry on I promise you can have your own room and your own phone."

This is a ploy, and I know it, but it is a tempting one. I have shared a room my whole life. To finally have a room to myself, complete with my own phone? I can feel my resolve disintegrating.

"A pink Princess style phone?" I ask.

"You bet," sporty Dad laughs and extends his hand for a shake.

And, yes, I shake on it.

No matter what I say, we will still move, so I think the better of arguing. I take comfort in being such an easy sell-out by picturing a sophisticated new life in Seattle with a private bedroom and my own phone.

"When do we move?" I ask, wanting to map out how many more troop meetings, fundraisers or badges I can muster with my dwindling days in Phoenix.

"I am going next week to look for a house and a job, then the rest of you will join me in August," light-hearted Daddy merrily replies.

Two months, I have just two months. My thoughts race ahead to all the packing, the explaining, yet another good-bye ceremony at my last troop meeting, being the new kid again at another new school. For the first time, it all seems insurmountable to me.

"Now, let's enjoy this Seattle food and look forward to our new adventure," my father toasts with his cocktail and we all reach out to clunk our cups of milk on his glass.

I think he's disappointed that we didn't regale him with a rousing chorus of "For He's A Jolly Good Fellow," because when I ask, "What is this anyway?"—while dubiously poking the meat around with my fork and watching it roll—as abruptly as he appeared, average-unnervingly-nice-Dad disappeared. In his place is my father, who drops his fork on his plate, the clanking sound halting the conversational buzz at The Beaman table.

He answers and then commands me,

"Scallops, which is a fancy name for fish eyeballs, now eat them and shut up."

In my short life, I have accumulated a great deal of useful knowledge.

I am certain that getting good grades can protect me from the vagaries of life. Additionally, I have badges to prove I know, among other things, how to cook, how to take photographs, how to camp, knit, swim, and ride horses. I have handwriting awards, blue ribbons for track, and a junior lifeguard patch.

Despite this storehouse of hard won wisdom, what I do not know is that fish do not officially have eyeballs.

Forced to eat six scallops at dinner, I go to bed and make myself sick to the point of dry heaves as I recall the gelatinous texture, opaque coloring, and downright cannibalism of eating another creature's eyes.

I never know whether each speedy run to the toilet is intended to purge myself of the offending food, or to rid myself of a bottomless sorrow.

The following morning, I know it will take more than my having earned the Creative Solutions badge for me to survive this next move.

It will take a miracle.

Why not explore the wet and wonderful world of water.

GIRL SCOUT BADGE BOOK

Water Fun

I am soaking wet. My swimsuit drips chlorinated water that lands on the Jolly Green Giant footprint rug in the bathroom at Doug Thatcher's house. I am inspecting my neck in the mirror. My pageboy hairdo only hangs down to my earlobes, so I have a clear view of the menacing mark that leaves Sharon Rayburn flabbergasted when she sees it. She almost screams and then hastily yanks me into this bathroom.

"That is the hugest, most vile hickey I have ever seen," Sharon's eyes are as big as hula hoops and her breath smells like the Jeno's sausage pizza we were happily gorging on only moments ago.

She is scaring me.

There is a pink blotch on my neck ... no, is it red? It's definitely turning purple. It's actually spreading right before my eyes. It looks like it's on the way to becoming the size of the giant footstep rug I am standing on.

"What is it? A what?" I fluster. I don't even know what I have and if it's catching. I begin shivering and my teeth are chattering. Not because I am soaked, but because I am afraid.

"It's a HICKEY," she whisper-shrieks, "and I am here to tell you, it's enormous."

"How did I get it? Is it from the pool chemicals?" I hazard a desperate guess.

At this, Sharon freezes. She moves her grave face several inches too close to mine, and bilging with the aroma of cheap pepperoni, says, in a voice several octaves lower than her previous screeches,

"What do you mean how did you get this?" Her eyes narrow, waiting for my reply.

The tension between us, coupled with the stench of her dinner, causes me to verp, a combination of vomit and burp, but I still manage to say, "I have never had this, this thing, whatever it is, will I be OK? Will it spread down the rest of my body? Is it contagious?"

Just two days before attending my going away party, my father had taken me to The Yellow Front Store to buy me a new swimming suit. My parents were not happy that I had left the cute, red plaid and denim suit at the high school pool, but offered to buy me a new one since this was a special occasion. In return, I promised to pack up the kitchen dishes, wrapping each carefully in the newspapers that were perpetually saved in piles for whenever the next moved occurred.

The Yellow Front was a Phoenix shopping institution, kind of like a hometown, but junkier, version of Kmart. It was a single story, concrete brick, two block long box of a building, and no surprise, the front was painted bright yellow. All the stores of early Phoenix didn't bother with clever names. It was Phil's Shoe Store. Or Vickie's Bra and Underwear Shop, The Eyeglass Place, Ed's Hot Dog House, or The Burger Chef. It was almost as if the vendors thought heat stroke had rendered every Phoenician unable to discern what a store carried unless it was spelled out for them.

Anyway, my father and I passed through the portals of Yellow Front and I happily waved good-bye to him. I assumed he would be heading to the cigarette or yard-work section as I turned toward the girlswear department.

Grabbing my hand, tenderly, my father walked with me and said,

"It's time you had a bikini."

I think the self-preservation section of my brain caused me to think he had said Binky. I was sorting this idea through my head while he continued,

"This is your going away party. You should wow them."

Now, my father only hit me in the face once, I was never hungry, I was never homeless, but I was, hundreds of times and in thousands of ways, rendered speechless and stymied by the things he said and did. Saying I would wow my friends by wearing a bikini qualified as one of these moments.

Besides, this desire for me to wow my pals by wearing a bikini comes from the same man who gifted me with the declaration, "Those pants make your rear end look two axe handles wide." I had bought a pink cowgirl shirt and matching pink jeans for rodeo day at school and thought I looked pretty good until I passed him on my way out the door and he issued his fashion critique which caused me to un-tuck my shirt, pull it down as far as it would go, and side step past my classmates all day long. They thought the hide-my-butt-shuffle was my homage to the square dance in keeping with the rodeo day theme.

And who could forget, certainly not me, that after complaining of a side ache for two days, my father and mother gave me Milk of Magnesia and sent me to bed. Then they stood outside my bedroom door and convened a staged conversation, intentionally loud enough for me to hear, that boiled down to,

Mother: "Do you think Ronda's side ache is serious?"

Father: "No, I think she is too chubby and that is what is making her side hurt."

No one in the desert was chubby, the heat melted any extra weight an adult might have and anyone under age fifteen looked like a tanned skeleton, including me. I knew as soon as I heard them they were just trying to get me to stop complaining and avoid having to take me to a real doctor.

Being at Yellow Front with my father and having him decide to shop for me was bad enough. The fact that he was also a key-carrying member of the Playboy club only made it downright alarming. I had seen copies of Playboy. I had seen the copies of my mother's *How To Belly Dance for Your Husband* and *How To Strip for Your Husband* LP albums. I had seen her parade in front of him naked. I had seen enough.

"Daddy, thank you, but, really, an ordinary two-piece will do. Or even a cute one piece, I am sure that would cost less, anyway," I try.

"Let your Daddy buy you your first bikini. It will be a special memory, like the first time we dance together someday. I still remember the first time I danced with my mother and you will remember this day like I remember that one," he said, totally convinced that he was right.

Let's go dancing and call this a day, I thought, looking at him and knowing he was right. I would never forget this. But par for our course, it was not the memory he would want me to have. My father thought that since I was his child, I would not only look like him, but my thoughts, translations, needs, wants, hopes, and goals would be his, too. I think it took him a long time ... alright, I think he never accepted the fact that I was not a clone or a pet because for most of my life I had been so agreeable and well behaved in order to get along with him.

I never argued, or fought back, and seldom stood up for myself, or my brother and sister. I am not sure what I was afraid of, but I was indeed afraid and did what as I was told because good scouts mind their parents. And I didn't want him not to love me. And I wanted his approval. And it's not like he asked me to act immorally or illegally. He just consistently told me to do things that did not feel right for me. Like buy a bikini.

My father steered me to the women's section, and from there, toward the swimsuits. Although I was as tall and developed as I was ever going to get by the seventh grade, and even though I had legitimately joined the lucky league of womanhood, it had never occurred to me to identify myself as a young woman. In my heart, I was a girl. In terms of maturity, I was a girl. And in terms of clothing for pool parties, I wanted to remain a girl.

"Let's see what we can do," my father said as he pushed through suits of many colors, some with built in bra cups, some with gold and silver threads as straps, all looking impossible to swim in, let alone wear. My father picked out three, one suit was made of a red scarf like material, one was a simple black, and one suit was navy blue and white polka dot. "Try these." He handed them to me. "I'll wait out here."

"That's OK, Daddy. You don't have to wait, I'll pick the best one and meet you up front," I prayed.

"No, no, don't be silly. This is a team effort. I want to see each of them on you and we'll pick together."

Knowing "we" meant he, I schlumped into the dressing room. I should be thankful for small favors, I told myself, it could be worse. He could come in with me.

Like Goldilocks, I dutifully tried on each suit and modeled for my father. The red one was too big. The black one was too small.

Visions of my mother's sparkling nipples and barely there underwear were dancing through my head as I stood for his judgment, and the same feeling of suffocating at the high school pool resurfaced.

The blue and white polka dot one was just right.

"Look at you, you look all grown up. You will be a big hit at your party."

My father was lit up and proud of the bikini. He turned to me at the cash register and, as he forked over the lavish amount of almost ten dollars said, "This is your badge of womanhood and I am so happy we could do this together. It's a special rite of passage we will always share."

I rode home holding the bag and wrestling with the same disturbing, violated sensation I had when I participated in a junior lifeguard class. And, to make matters worse, I also had the same sullied-in-Biblical proportions feeling I got from my brother.

I had been on a summer swim team since fifth grade. So, it seemed like a good idea to become a lifeguard. I could see myself spending my teen summers in a regulation Red Cross Lifeguard suit, my nose covered in thick, white zinc oxide. Plus, I would get my own whistle and I could blow it and make other people follow the rules. The job was custom made for someone like me.

I signed up for the junior lifeguard course at our local pool during spring break and arrived with the registration form signed by my father and our doctor, who were, of course, one and the same.

The teacher was a senior lifeguard named Benny. Benny was short, had long dark hair, and a black beard—which should have been my first clue that something depraved would happen. Everyone knows a prerequisite for being a male lifeguard is to be tall, blonde, and look like a movie star.

All went well the first day, until Benny chose me, from among the other dozen or so students, to rescue and save. I wanted to die. He pulled me, on my back, with his arm around my neck, out of the pool, and gave me mouth-to-mouth resuscitation. With his soaked beard, it felt like I was being saved by a soppy Brillo pad. He also did chest pump compressions that were supposed to demonstrate how to help a victim survive.

I walked home that day feeling like a victim and thinking I should drown Benny.

It has been said that strengths over-extended become weakness, and so it was that "drowning in optimism" I went to the lifesaving class the next day. Yep, when it came time for chest blocks, Benny again beckoned. This time, on dry land, Benny demonstrated how to place both hands against the drowning person's chest, meaning mine, to block them from grabbing the rescuer and pulling him down. He was a thorough teacher and showed the class how to put their hands on my chest four more times. He then jumped in the pool and told me to join him so we could instruct the class how to block and drag a person in the water.

I jumped in, swam to Benny, and began flailing, as he asked me to do. When he came to "save me" and deliver a chest block, I beat him to it and with full force delivered a crotch block. As the other students swam toward Benny to rescue him, I swam to the steps, climbed out of the pool, and never returned.

All my Water Fun wasn't centered around swimming pools. One afternoon after playing neighborhood softball, I took an early shower to get cleaned up for my scout meeting later that night. I was washing my hair when I heard a loud thump on the side of the house. I stood straight up, my ear cocked to the left of the shower, listening, waiting to maybe hear it again, but did not. So, I went back to scrubbing, turned my back to the showering water, and tilted my head to rinse out the shampoo. Suddenly a shadow in the outline of a head, and then the silhouette of shoulders appeared at the heavily frosted window that was eye level on the shower wall.

I screamed, hit the floor of the shower, and grabbed the shower curtain to wrap around me as I quickly climbed out. I lay on the floor, still screaming and terrified, but knowing I needed a plan of escape. My mother was not home, but my sister came running up the stairs and into the bathroom. I screamed at her to call the police and I pulled my shorts and shirt on, ran to the kitchen to get a knife, and told her to stay in our room. There was sheer pandemonium and emergency defense plans being shouted throughout the house. I scooched the dresser in front of the door to barricade us from the menacing stranger attempting to get in through a tiny second-floor shower window.

"Where is our brother?" I yelled in hysterics. My sister cried out that he was playing in the backyard.

"Don't let the bad man get him, Ronda, save him."

I stopped cold. "Wait just a cotton picking minute," I said to her.

I stood for a moment in our fortified room and considered this bit of information before I pushed the dresser away from the door and stepped into the hall, looking back at my sister and telling her to "Stay here" before I re-closed the door.

With the murder of my little brother on my mind, I cautiously made my way, kitchen knife in hand, out to the deck that was off the second-story living room of our house. I looked to my left, toward the direction of the scene of the crime. I saw our ladder positioned right beneath the bathroom window. And, not to my surprise, I saw my brother standing at the bottom, holding his sides because he was laughing so hard.

"You are a psycho, a pure psycho," I yelled. And I knew psychos. My parents had taken us to see the movie *Psycho* at the drive-in when I was only five, making him four and my sister three. During the knifing in the shower scene, I was head down on the floor of the backseat, with them on top of me, our Necco wafers spilling around us like tiddly-winks.

"What is the matter with you?" I screamed at him and waved the knife hoping to look maniacal.

He looked up, grinned, and defended himself by saying,

"Welcome to the Bates Motel."

With Hugh Hefner as a father and the star of *Psycho* as a brother, it's no wonder I now find myself in trouble wearing a teeny weeny navy blue polka dot bikini, staring at my hickey, with Sharon Rayburn breathing down my neck.

"David Twyman and I were necking, that's it, necking is all we were doing!" I explain.

"Necking?" Sharon repeats, incredulous. "Ronda, he was SUCKING."

Wanting desperately to be the big hit my father is sure I will be—and more than a little confused about bodies, boys, and bikinis—I agreed to let David Twyman sit next to me and "neck" while everyone else paired up to make out. I did think his little mouth movements were strange, but I didn't have to touch him anywhere, and except for his head on my shoulder and his lips on my neck, he wasn't touching me anywhere. I had heard the term necking, but had never really known what it was, until tonight. *What is all the fuss about?* I think, feeling my decision to just neck had been a good, if not an altogether boring, one. No one would call me a party pooper and I didn't have to kiss anyone back.

"He was sucking my neck? Why? Why in the world would someone do that?" Now it is me who is incredulous.

"Gawd, don't you know anything?" Sharon laughs. She opens the bathroom door before I can stop her and yells for Pam Keasey to come "Help Ronda."

Meanwhile, back at the party in my honor, everyone who simply made out is now having ice cream, playing "Marco Polo" and "Jump or Dive" in the pool. Doug's parents are lighting the bamboo tiki torches. Everyone is having a seemingly good time—including that little hoover, David Twyman.

Pam, a fellow scout, rushes over and wedges herself through the tiny crack of an opening that Sharon allows and stands with us in the small bathroom with the giant fuzzy footprint rug on the ground. No one says a word. Sharon points at my neck, Pam covers her mouth with her hand, and I start sobbing.

"I've never seen a hickey like that," Pam finally shudders.

How is it everyone but me knows what this spreading stigmata is called?

"How ... many ... have you se ... eeen? I ask in between blubbering and shivering.

"Lots. The arcade workers at the State Fair always have them."

This is comforting.

"We've got to get you out of here without anyone seeing your neck," Pam continues, proving that a friend in need is a friend indeed. "Sharon, go call Ronda's parents and tell them the party is ending, tell them she isn't calling because ... umm ... because everyone is saying good-bye to her and crying ... that's it, everyone is saying good-bye, she's sad and ready to leave, so please come get her now."

"Got it," Sharon says. "What's the number?" She looks at me intent on remembering it.

"944-8190" I reply bleakly, wishing I knew another number so I could go home somewhere else.

"I got it," Sharon opens the door and ekes out, "I'll call."

Pam asks me where my towel is and I tell her I left it out on the porch. "It says 'The Egyptian Motel'" on it I sniff, remembering my innocent days of half-price summer swimming at Phoenix motels with my family. Oh how I miss the unsullied days and the comfort of my peculiar little family, I think, becoming nostalgic and nauseous.

She says sternly, "We need to wrap you up in it, all the way around your neck and keep you hidden until we can get you to the driveway. I'll be right back, don't move."

That's rich, don't move. If I wasn't moving, if I didn't come to this going away party, if I was swimming instead of necking, if, if, if … then none of this would have happened. I stand staring into the mirror transfixed by the marked, soaked, sad, stranger with the long wet bangs looking back at me.

Pam and Sharon wrap me like a mummy, scout the trail to the driveway, and when the coast is clear, walk me outside and wait with me until my parents arrive.

I climb into the backseat of the car and wave good-bye. My mind is shifting gears during the drive home. I cannot imagine what I will possibly say to minimize my lost maidenhood. And, uncharacteristically chatty and interested, my parents pepper me with questions.

"Did you have a good time?"

"Uh-huh."

"Did anyone else have a new bikini?"

"Nuh-uh."

"Did you play games?"

"Uh-huh."

"Did you win any prizes?"

Boy, did I ever, I think but only reply, "Uh-huh."

The hickey is too big to hide, even if they don't see it, my sister will since I can't exactly stay wrapped in a towel forever. How long will it look like this? Can I claim it's a terrible bruise? Maybe maintain that I was playing "Jump or Dive," and I thought the call would be "Jump," but when they yelled "Dive," I contorted mid-air in such a way to make a dive that I hit this side of my neck on the diving board? What if instead, I go to the pool tomorrow and get really sunburned? Yes, a sunburn will hide it! A second degree burn will be a small price to pay not to have to tell my father that a boy I hardly know spent the evening sucking my neck.

"We're home," my parents say, more for reasons of identification rather than comfort and habit.

As we pull into the carport of our modest pale blue, brick home, I pull my bikini-ed and hickey-ed self out of the backseat, and head into the house, my rubber thongs flip flopping me toward my doom.

Within moments of entering our house, I break down crying and tell my parents something terrible has happened.

"What? What is it, Ronda? What happened?" They are very alarmed and stand close to me in the dimly lit hallway.

I unwind myself from Pam and Sharon's custom camouflage job and turn my head to the left to reveal the recently acquired death mark.

"What did you do?" is, not surprisingly, the first question out of my father's mouth as my mother sucks all the air out of the hallway.

To my credit, I do try the truth first.

"I didn't know what I was doing, I didn't know what was happening, some boy had his head on my shoulder ..."

"SOME BOY! You let someone near enough to do this and it's just some boy? Who, who did this to you?" My father is plenty angry, but I'm unable to tell at whom ... me ... or the boy who used my neck as a straw.

"And don't tell me you didn't know what was going on, how could you not know you had a barnacle adhesived to your neck?"

OK, it's me in trouble.

"Ronda, your father gave me one of those, but I was sixteen and it wasn't nearly as big as yours," my mother adds, making it sound like a present, or a contest.

"You better tell us who did this, you better tell me how it happened, and you better start now," my father warns as he leads me into the living room. I start to sit down but my mother yells, "Don't sit down, your suit is damp."

Since the truth is not setting me free, I proceed to engage in a series of hall-of-fame worthy tall tales that make any lies from my diary seem like the work of a preschooler.

First I try the, "a bunch of guys jumped the fence while everyone else was in the house except me, they pinned me down while one sucked on my neck. And when he was finished, they all jumped back over the fence and ran down the alley before anyone from the party could catch them."

This will end the tortuous questioning. "Poor kid, so clearly desirable that boys are jumping fences to get at her" they will think and then sooth my nerves by fixing me a hot chocolate.

This approach does not work.

Only because my father wants to call the Thatcher household to find out why they have not chaperoned this party more carefully and ask them, "are you aware of what happened to Ronda?" due to their neglect.

So, in an even more heightened state of panic, I claim there is a "club" forming and to belong we all have to get these marks, sort of a red badge of courage, if you will.

"Every girl at the party got a hickey?" my mother asks, this time making it sound like a door prize.

"Yes," I reply and then, without provocation or premeditation, I say "even Pam and Sharon."

"Are you trying to tell me that some boy gave homely Sharon Rayburn a hickey?" my father says suspiciously.

Homely? I never noticed, I've only noticed she was—and at this point I know the story I am telling will place the emphasis on the *was*—my friend.

My father stares at me for a moment, and then asks me to

go get my address book. I stare back, attempting to glean a clue as to what he might be thinking or planning to do.

I hand over the book and he walks to the phone. He calls Pam's house, he calls Sharon's house. I sit perfectly still and soberly quiet as I watch him talk to innocent parents who are now speeding over to the party to check their daughter's necks. I don't speak up, I don't stop the dialing, I just sit there until the calls are finished and simply say, "May I please go put on my pajamas?"

Within the hour the returns are in. No one else has a hickey. And no one else at the party will be speaking to me for the rest of the summer, or more to the point, no one is gonna miss me when I move away.

I have to wear a turtleneck for almost two months during my last summer in Phoenix. I stay hidden inside my room most days and if my mother asks me to go out to get the mail or sweep the sidewalk, once outside I blink up at the sun like the "Birdman of Alcatraz" and sweat profusely. Neighbors who get a brief look at me grow concerned and bring dinners over to help my mother care for her apparently seriously ill child.

Not one friend from my school or my troop comes by to see me, not that I blame them. When we finally pack up for our move, my neck is clear, as are my goals. For the first time, I consider moving as a form of rescue and reinvention. I will not pack the accumulated demerits and red marks I have accrued in Phoenix. The opportunity to create a new and improved version of myself in a different state gives me a jittery happiness that feels the way I have imagined being a teenager would feel.

Winning this badge, I find myself relishing the idea of different Water Fun living in Seattle ... a place too rainy to wear a swimsuit.

The journey you will make to become a teenager
is an exciting and challenging one.

GIRL SCOUT BADGE BOOK

Becoming a Teenager

I am trying really hard not to over-react—which is never my strong suit. I am distressed just looking at the chocolate brown naugahyde vest and matching dirndl skirt my mother has purchased, from God knows where, and is so delighted to give me. I am wondering what to say, what can I say, without hurting her feelings.

I flash back to the cute gray felt skirt she bought me last Valentine's Day. The full skirt came with a built-in slip and two big red felt hearts on the left. I loved it!

Until Sue Thornton walks up to me at lunch saying, not unkindly,

"That's my skirt."

"You have one too? Don't you love it?" I twirl and whoosh.

"No, I mean that skirt you are wearing is mine. My mother made it for me a couple of years ago for a play I was in. I was the Queen of Hearts in *Alice in Wonderland*," she smiles sweetly. "We gave it to the Goodwill when the play was over."

I smile, weakly, and in an effort to be funny I curtsy, pulling the sides of my new, old skirt out as I dip my knees. Sue walks away regally.

I never wore that skirt again.

I mange a heartfelt, "You shouldn't have," when I take the plastic outfit from my mother, which could not have been a more truthful sentiment.

"I never expected this," I continue, holding the hanger and bearing the outfit up and at arms length away, hoping it might look better at a distance.

It doesn't.

I should have been much more specific when stating that I longed for a leather skirt and vest ... leather ... I am sure I said leather. But it seems in the strange, new leather outfit world of ninth grade Seattle, I am doomed to be an imitation for the real thing. Everyone here is pale, pasty, and plump. The girls wear knee high socks over their nylons and navy blue jackets called *P* Coats. Maybe it's Pea Coats? I have no idea what the *P* stands for or why the *H* they wear them.

The school hallways are indoor corridors and tennis is played in an overheated canvas tent called a "Bubble." Crab and lobster is served at fast food places, probably scallops, too, though I never get close enough to any of these places to find out.

At my first school here, which I attend for two months, there is not a Girl Scout uniform to be seen, nor any troop meeting information posted on a bulletin board. There is a group called a "Drill Team" advertising they need "Interested Girls."

My tenure as a Girl Scout has taught me to join, to raise my hand, to explore, and commit. The Girl Scouts engender "Interested Girls," so naturally I go to the first meeting of this club even though I don't have a whit of an idea about what I will be drilling.

"You mean you have to try out to march in a straight line down the football field?" my father laughs that night at dinner.

"I know, I know," I sigh, "I am sure there is more to it than that."

There isn't.

I do make the Lake Washington High School Drill team. My knee position at the full march is noted as being, "elevated without showing off" and I march in a straight line for two games before we move to another house in another school district.

At the next school, it is too late in the fall to try out for cheerleader or drill team, but I do try out for the school play and win the role of Becky Thatcher in *Tom Sawyer*. Learning my lines, rehearsing, wearing costumes and make-up, pretending to be someone else, the whole thing feels like a call from my distant grown up life. Rather than being the *Miracle Worker*, I can probably star as her—as well as many other heroines. This will be my contribution to mankind. And talk about awards! I can already see the Oscar gleaming on my someday mantle.

"I'd like to be an actress," I announce theatrically.

"No, you don't," my father puts his fork down at another dinner in another house.

"How do you know what I want to be? I do want to be an actress," I argue.

"First of all, you never think of, say, or do anything that I've never thought, said, or done. It's an impossibility."

"That makes no sense, you are not me, how do you know what I think or feel, or what I want to do?"

"I know because I've lived first. It's my job to know. So, no, you don't want to be an actress. Not really. If you wanted to be an actress you would be acting any chance you got. You would be in plays and shows and auditioning for any and all chances to act. You've never done that, and being in one play doesn't qualify as wanting to be an actress."

"This is ridiculous. You won't even give me a ride to school in the pouring rain so of course you won't want to haul me to drama class, rehearsals, costume fittings, or whatever it is an actress needs." I am infuriated.

"If you really want to be an actress, you'll find a way to work it out, you'll make it happen with or without me," he replies, smugly.

"Oh yeah?" My hormonal steam is gurgling inside me, my definition of "self" is taking shape, and I've lost my temper—and maybe even my fear of him ... and it's only taken thirteen years.

"You wanna know what kind of actress I am, you wanna know how good I am at playing a role? I have vast experience in acting because, for your information, I've been acting all along as if I like being your daughter."

As soon as I say it, I am sorry. It doesn't feel good to say, it feels ugly and mean, and not worthy of the kind of person I want to be.

And I might as well have hit him with a two-by-four. In fact, my father looks like he has been thwacked right across his formerly smug, all-knowing face.

The world stops, the dining room disappears, and it seems like it is only the two of us alone on the planet. It appears to me as if he is moving and speaking in slow motion. He puts his fork down, looks square into my face, and sounding like he is holding back tears, his throat clenching, he simply says, "I ... am ... sorry ... you ... feel ... that ...way." Then, delicately, he folds his napkin and places it to the left of his plate, pushes his chair away from the table, and walks—as if bearing the weight of the world—toward his bedroom.

I draw in a breath. The dining room reappears, my brother and sister are shaking their heads at me, and my mother is saying something about how I need to go apologize to "Daddy."

Taking his lead, I also leave the table and go to the room I still share with my sister. The house with my own room hasn't yet appeared. I sit down to weigh my options.

I am sure I will have to apologize, I am sure he won't make it easy, and I am sure this is the beginning of growing up. Wearing pink lipstick on the sly, taking my socks off once I get to school, letting boys think they've beat me in a race or tennis game, pretending I don't know the answer so a boy can think he is the smart one—all are petty preludes to what becoming a teen means for me, which is finding my voice. And, in an unanticipated turn, my teenage voice is vocalizing lonely, mad, confused, sad, stunted, and vengeful. Not exactly the list of attributes found on the Girl Scout laws.

Sitting alone in my bedroom, I picture my father down the hall sitting in his room, both of us hurt, angry, and feeling misunderstood. Why did I say I didn't like being his daughter? Is it really how I feel? I think of my friend Jan Simonds and her dad. He smokes a pipe, wears cardigan sweaters, and calls her "Kitten" just like the dad on *Father Knows Best*. Or what about Norma Andersen whose dad is a mailman and sells Amway on the side? He is portly and laughs easily. My father called him a "simpleton" after he came to our house to show his new product line. And I think about all the dads on television who adore their TV daughters. I want to be adored, I want my father to hold my hand and listen compassionately to my small problems and bigger crisis. I want his face to light up when I come into the room.

I continue to reflect that there are plenty of reasons for my outburst, and sure, my relationship with my father is not what I want, or need ... but, I tell myself, it's not like he has a list of requirements he can follow to earn a "Good Dad" badge. And, left to his own devices, he has done many good things, not the least of which include giving me food—liver and scallops aside—and a roof over my head ... many different roofs.

I think of my final summer in Phoenix when my father, though upset about the lies I told regarding my behavior at the going away party, invited me to swim laps with him in the morning before anyone else was up.

I like the way my father calls me "Wilma Worker" when he asks me to do a chore because he knows I will do it well.

I know it is a sign of affection when he refers to me as "Nana," which was the way I pronounced my name until I got old enough to manage the *R*.

I like that he thought my third grade teacher, Mrs. Lauman,

was wrong about me and wrote a nasty note to her.

I am touched he believes me enough to want to call Doug Thatcher's parents about the supposed mob that jumped the fence to give me a hickey.

I like that, when I fell in love with the Edsel automobile, he brought home a plastic model of it for me to put together.

It is a sign of interest in my future that while other girls had dolls, he gave me a white toy truck with an orange painted on the side so I could pretend I was a business owner making my juice deliveries.

I appreciate the important stories he told me. Like the one about the Mexican jumping bean only jumping as high as the lid of the jar it's placed in. Even when the lid is finally removed the bugs never jump any higher the rest of their lives, "Just like people," he says, "most of their barriers are imagined."

Deep down I feel respected by the fact that he never lets me win when we play anything from chess to craps. Because when I win, I know it is really me who wins.

It is my father who puts up the tetherball pole in our back-yards so I can practice and remain the reigning queen of the game no matter where we move.

He goads me into defending my point of view by always—and I mean always—arguing the opposite side regardless of the topic.

And it is my father who constantly challenges my capabilities and dares me to overcome my adversities.

"There are two sides to every coin," he often tells me. And here I am, wearing a badge of pride about being a good scout, a bright student, and a solid citizen on the outside, but on the inside I am a liar, con artist, and let's face it, a girl whose latest aquatic antics rate me one short step above carnie worker.

Who knows, as a daughter I might not be what he wants or needs, either, I conclude, but at least he never says out loud that he is sorry he is my father.

Yep, becoming a teenager, it seems to me now, means not only finding my voice, but using it in the right way. Which means, in this case, I have to apologize.

I walk to the family room and find my father and mother having a cigarette and watching television. No lights are on and the smoke hovering above their heads looks like two little ghosts waiting for instructions about who to go haunt next. Little Joe Cartwright from *Bonanza* is reflected in my father's glasses; I cannot see his eyes.

"Daddy, I am sorry I said I don't like being your daughter."

He does not look at me, he does not get up to turn down the volume of the TV, he does not respond for at least three minutes. I stand there, looking at him, like a dog waiting for the occasional, but perpetually hoped for, treat.

Finally, when he does speak, he says quietly and with no inflection, "I have told you before that words can hurt more than actions, you can never take back a bad thing you say. I will never forget what you said to me and I will think of your angry statement often. I suggest you choose your words more carefully from here on out, not just with me, but with everyone you interact with. Goodnight."

I am sure I am not the first, or last, teen to think, "of all the hypocritical, double standard, phony, two-faced, 'do as I say, not as I do' speeches, this one tops them all. He never apologies to anyone, he thinks he's always right. Well, he's not always right. I can't wait to get out of here. Thank God I only have five more years until I am on my own. The man can't even throw me a bone. Who does he think he is, making me stand here like this? This is the last time I apologize to him for anything. He'll be sorry, oh yes, when I get that Oscar, or win the Nobel Peace Prize, or whatever I do. He'll be sorry because I won't be saying 'Thank You' to him for anything. That's for sure. He'll regret that he wasn't nicer to me. He'll miss me, and he'll be wracked with regrets, he'll see ..."

But all I say is "Goodnight."

We move a third time, to my third school of ninth grade, right after my stage debut as Becky Thatcher. The third times the charm and my father makes good on his promise—I get my own room!

And phone. Which is pointless because I have no friends to call in this new state full of people I don't know anyway.

My room is austere—a roll away bed, a dresser, and a milk carton for a nightstand, but it is mine, all mine. I am saving up my allowance, birthday money, and babysitting income so I can buy the materials to paint the walls pink, get a red bedspread, and cover the milk crate in pink and red flowered Contact paper. My private quarters will out-do the Barbie Dream House bedroom when I'm finished with it.

On the day the pink Princess phone is installed, my parents come in to watch my inaugural call.

"I don't have anyone to call," I whine, "I don't know anyone."

"Why don't you call Grandma?" my mother suggests.

"That's pitiful," I cry, "my first call on my own phone is to my Grandmother? It's downright pathetic. Should I invite her to my first sleepover, too?"

"That's enough," my father says.

"Yeah, that's enough moving from place to place," I push. "Do you have any idea what it's like to keep going to new schools, to always be the one trying to make people want to be your friend?" I say, working myself into a nasal-y, high-pitched yowl.

"Why should *you* want anyone to be your friend?" he asks.

"Well, let me think, I respond unpleasantly, "how about so I have someone besides my grandmother to call?"

"You're missing the point," he remains calm, "*they* should want to be your friend."

"What are you talking about?" I say, "I'm never anywhere long enough to get a desk assignment, let alone have anyone want to be my friend."

"Wherever you go," he lectures, "you should conduct your-self in a manner that draws positive attention and makes people think, 'it would be great to know her.' Someone with your social skills can make that happen instantly."

My father recently gave me a copy of his favorite book, *How to Win Friends and Influence People*. I read and liked it, but I am now all too familiar with his Dale Carnegie approach to parenting and I am unmoved by his attempt at inspiration.

"What skills? All I'm trained for is packing and unpacking," I complain.

What my parents obviously do not understand is that

fitting in at high school is arbitrary and capricious, at best. Anyone's chance to be accepted can be shot in an instant by something as simple as wearing the wrong clothes—or in my case clothes that once belonged to another classmate or are fake leather—or packing a deviled ham or liverwurst sandwich for lunch. What is liverwurst anyway and, more importantly, whom is my father kidding? Making friends in ninth grade, in any grade, is a delicate maneuver. Friendships can take months, if not years to cultivate. And, in turn, one false move, or stupid story, or misunderstood joke can ruin what has taken weeks or months to develop.

Take for example, my badminton debacle ...

Just before I moved to house number three in the Pacific Northwest, I had invited myself to play some basketball with a couple of girls my age who were dribbling on the courts after school. I introduced myself and asked if I could join the game. All agreed and we were having fun until a group of senior boys from the high school blasted onto the courts and told us to get lost. "The court is ours, it's not a little girls game anyway, beat it."

One of them actually shoved me.

He is cute, I thought, standing on the sidelines watching them play, but not cute enough to push me ... that was uncalled for and out of bounds.

My newfound girlfriends were complaining about the foul play, yet continued to stand on the sidelines doing nothing.

I have to take action, I thought. I needed to retaliate, but nothing so bad that they hit me or something, and nothing that would make the cute boy think I was a loser, and I wanted to save my new friends' game so they become fast friends ... this moment called for a big play.

And that's when "genius" struck. I yelled to whoever was listening, hoping that the girls and the cute boy heard me, "I will be right back, don't you guys go anywhere, I have something to say to you." I threatened and pointed at the boys on the courts, and then bounded away.

I ran up two flights of stairs, outside to the parking lots, cut across the baseball diamond, climbed the chain link fence, dropped into a stranger's backyard, loped across their yard and down two more streets, before finally running up our driveway thinking, *Man, Washington is hilly, this would have taken half the time and effort in Phoenix.* I found, then I rummaged through the "College Sports Box" and located what I was looking for—the badminton game. I removed the shuttlecock and with it firmly in my hand, ran back the way I came, landing courtside a good twenty minutes later to find, amazingly, everyone right where I left them. The boys were still playing basketball and the girls were watching the boys play basketball.

Panting, sweaty, and with high anticipation of saving the day and sealing new friendships, I strolled to the middle of the court. I looked back at my newest friends and hollered, "Watch this."

The boys stopped dribbling and before they could yell at me to "Beat it," I beat them to the punch and said,

"We are mad at you for kicking us off the court. My friends and I don't take this kind of treatment lightly and here's what we think of you, here's what we want to say to you,"

And then I tossed the birdie high up above my head and let in land, silently and lightly, at my feet.

"We are flipping you the bird," I said, nodding my head and crossing my arms in front of me in a defiant "Take that" kind of stance. "Get it? Flipping you the bird," I said to make sure they appreciated my highly evolved sense of humor.

To say that the boys laughed would be putting it mildly, they are probably still laughing. And not with me, they were laughing at me. To say that my new friends avoided me like the plague from then on would also be putting it mildly.

❧

So, no, I know, even more than my father or Dale Carnegie does, that making new friends is never easy. If, like me, you wear a classmate's recycled skirt, talk to support poles in the breezeway, think you're as funny as Red Skelton or move every three months, it's even trickier.

"Why don't you make some posters that say 'Ronda is Coming' or 'Who is Ronda?' and put them up before school starts one morning to get the other students curious about you?" my mother suggests.

Swell. Instantly, my stay-at-home mother has become a marketing expert.

"A poster? Saying I'm coming to their school? Oh, they'd be curious alright, like people gathered at a car wreck."

"No, no, really, this could work. Like a billboard. Or you could do a series of small signs down the hall like those Burma Shave signs along the highway ... only with your name and cute little sayings on them." She keeps going and offers, "Be A Man. Look for Ronda Beaman."

"Mother, I am not going to do it."

"It was Daddy's slogan when he ran for student body president, BE A MAN, vote BEAMAN!" she cheered. "He won."

I should have known.

"Ronda," my father pipes in, "it never takes you longer than five minutes to meet and make a new friend. I have seen you do it time and time again."

"OK," I reply, "so in less than five minutes you think I can make people understand the benefit of knowing me and make them feel better for knowing me ... which means I need to be a prostitute or a drug dealer," I suggest.

"You'll think of something, you always do," my father finishes.

As they left my room, my mother turns around and says,

"Call Grandma."

If there is an advantage to moving, it is that you get noticed. I've spent my entire thirteen-year-old life trying to get famous and/or discovered, so I consider "noticed" at least a good start.

Being the new student at three high schools often gets me a seat up front, even if it isn't alphabetical. This alone opens an uncharted territory of friendships with kids whose names don't end in A or B.

Being new in class also means I can take longer to turn in my homework assignments. The teachers want to give me time to catch up—each teacher at each new school always believes that their class is tougher and better than the classroom I was in previously.

And, in each new neighborhood, young mothers can smell

a potential babysitter a mile away. Thirteen is considered a perfect age to care for someone else's child; too young to have boyfriends who want to come visit, but old enough to make a bologna sandwich. Within the first month of being in our latest house I'm harvesting a thriving clientele of women who want to get out of the house for an hour here, an hour there.

Just two doors down is Mrs. Weiskind. She is somewhat famous because her husband owns Weiskind's Jewelry in the mall. She works there every Saturday and offers me a weekly job watching her baby boy.

This is just the monetary bump I need to complete my room remodel and buy that red bedspread! I happily accept.

Every pal, every Girl Scout, every girl I know who's ever babysat shares stories of looking through the drawers, cabinets, closets, and fridge of their employers. It is an unspoken, but universal, part of the job. In fact, it is part of the educational component of the job. In addition to learning how nasty it is to change a diaper or how turning the clocks throughout the house ahead doesn't guarantee that you get a six-year-old to go to bed, a babysitter learns what being an adult holds in store by rifling through the drawers and cupboards of their employer—leaving me plenty glad to be thirteen.

While babysitting I read my first *Playboy* magazine (disturbing), taste my first whiskey (disgusting), and wobble in my first high heels (disappointing).

Mrs. Weiskind's is a good job and I like it. I'm missing Saturday chores at my house, the potato chips and coke are plentiful, baby Weiskind sleeps a lot, and I try on lots of the jewelry I find when snooping through her stuff.

One afternoon while the baby is napping, I go out to the garage to sit in the driver's seat of her husband's MG sports car. I don't do anything, just pretend to drive it through the English countryside with Davy Jones in the passenger seat singing "Daydream Believer" and holding hands with me.

While laughing at something witty and charming that Davy says, I notice a group of brown paper bags stuffed with clothes, labeled "Goodwill," lined up on the left side of the washer and dryer.

Fair game, I think, bidding adieu to my favorite Monkee. I begin sorting through the clothes, stopping when I come across a cute pair of culottes, that tricky piece of apparel that looks like a skirt but is really shorts.

I go in the house, slip out of my pants, and try on Mrs. Weiskind's culottes. Although not a perfect fit, I don't have a pair of culottes so I stuff hers into my homework bag then watch TV until the baby wakes up.

That Friday I wear the Mrs. Weiskind-Goodwill-culottes to school. At the end of the day the school bus pulls up to my stop, which is directly across the street from Mrs. Weiskind's house. She is out getting her mail. I hop off the bus, walk in front of it toward my house, and wave hello to her, not even thinking about my fashion faux pas.

Mrs. Weiskind freezes at her mailbox not returning my wave or my hello, but her eyes follow me all the way to my front door.

I quickly (and frantically) change my clothes, but I'm not as quick as Mrs. Weiskind, who knocks on our front door within thirty seconds. My mother answers and I hear mumbling ... I am thankful there is no yelling, and then I hear the door close.

By now I've changed into play clothes, ready to return Mrs. Weiskind's outcast culottes and apologize for not waiting to pick them up at Goodwill.

I hear my mother's footsteps coming down the hall. They stop at my closed door. She doesn't knock but she opens the door slowly. She barely steps in my room and only asks, "Did you do it? Did you take Mrs. Weiskind's culottes?"

"Mother, it was a Goodwill throwaway, she didn't want it. It's not like I stole it."

"Did you ask her if you could have it?"

"No, I didn't even think about it ..." I trail off.

"If you didn't ask her, that's stealing. Wait here until Daddy gets home." With that she closes the door as slowly as she opened it.

My father gets home early and comes directly into my room. I'm sitting on my bed with my back up against the wall. He takes a seat at the foot of the bed and turns to face me.

"Why? I buy you clothes, you have everything you need. Why would you do something like this?" His tone is serious, his face cheerless.

"I didn't mean to," I scramble to sit up and closer to him, "it was junk, I took her cast offs. I didn't think it was a big deal," I plead.

"If you do not ask, if you do not tell, it is stealing. You know that. It's not the worth of the item, the kind of item, or the potential demise of the item, if it's not yours and you take it, you are stealing."

"Yes, sir."

"Ronda, you are the apple of my eye and it hurts and disappoints me that you did this. I have to think about what I am going to do about this situation. I'll be back, you wait here." And with that he leaves my room for about two hours.

Why does it take a misdemeanor for him to say I am the apple of his eye? Why doesn't he say it when I earn a badge or win an election or get an "A"?

When he returns, still dressed in his suit and tie, he lays out my punishment as if he has been rehearsing the lines.

"Tomorrow morning I want you to get up and get dressed as if you are going to school. You will not, of course, be babysitting for Mrs. Weiskind tomorrow, you have lost the privilege of that job and she, understandably, doesn't want you to work for her anymore. I will pick you up at 8 a.m. here in your room. When you steal from one person, it makes you suspect for all people. So, you are going to go to the door of everyone in the neighborhood, and you will pay a visit to everyone within our block you have babysat for, tell them what you did, and let them know that you did not steal anything from them ... and I am assuming you have not taken anything else from anyone else?"

He looks at me as if prepared for some more bad news.

"No, Daddy, I didn't take anything else, I swear. But can't I be grounded? I already lost my job. That's already a punishment. I've learned my lesson, really ... I have more than learned my lesson."

"I will see you in the morning, 8 a.m. sharp. You better prepare your apology to the people you'll see tomorrow."

No dinner, no breakfast. I'm not to come out until I walk

the plank. I'm in solitary confinement in my longed for private room. I organize my closet, I finish homework, and I sneak out when everyone else goes to bed so I can get some water.

I don't need my alarm clock because I don't fall asleep. I'm dressed and ready when my father arrives at my door. He is quiet and only asks me if I know what I'm going to say to our neighbors. I reply queasily that I do.

We go to eleven different houses, stand on eleven different front porches, ring the bell or knock on eleven different doors—starting with Mrs. Weiskind—and issue eleven of the same explanations and apologies with tears, and deep regret. My father, dressed in a business suit and tie, stands right next to me. He walks up each driveway I encounter, climbs every step I have to climb, waits for each door to open and watches me in each painful re-telling of my life of unintended crime. It is brutal, humbling, and emotionally devastating to hear myself admit again and again that I have taken something that doesn't belong to me.

The fact that my father doesn't wait for me at the curb, or send me up to each door alone, the fact that he stands by me, only makes me more ashamed of myself and more respectful of him.

When we finish canvassing the neighborhood, when I've shared my last thievery story, we walk home in silence. He changes his clothes, grabs a beer, makes a liverwurst sandwich and sits down to watch *Wide World of Sports*.

Back in my room, I lie down, exhausted from the emotional workout and think, for once I am actually learning what he wants me to learn. Sure, I already know the part about stealing being wrong, and now I know even if something is in a trash can, don't take it without asking. Fine. Got it. The Weiskind lesson, for me, is knowing my father will stand by me. Today his actions, both wise and kind, spoke louder than his words.

As a teenager I am spending more time in front of a mirror, yet I have never been less sure of who I am. Am I Girl Scout or thief, friend or foe, trustworthy or con artist, someone genuine or merely a cheap imitation?

I have badgered for accomplishment, friendship, love, and belonging—often in less than honorable methods and employing ways and means never condoned by the Girl Scouts. In my all out effort to make merit, I have accumulated badges but lost my way.

Even with a badge to prove I am Becoming a Teenager, I'm still a long way from becoming who I want to be.

When you have a good opinion of yourself,
you take positive risks and avoid negative ones.
You make and keep friends, and you're successful in life!

GIRL SCOUT BADGE BOOK

Being My Best

I am center stage, on national television, holding a micro-phone, and singing "Sweet Home Alabama." My name is in lights six feet high and flashing on a multi-colored electronic billboard. Ten thousand people tried out for this hit show, but I won the audition.

"Lord, I'm coming home to you ..."

The nine producers of the hit show who interviewed me loved my story about auditioning for my parents, "You mean you didn't even pass an audition with your own parents? That's hilarious!"

They appreciate my chutzpah at wanting a chance to rewrite my life story about making music by singing in front of the country on prime time.

My sons are asked to share the stage with me because we were named America's Most Creative Family.

"That will add a human interest slant for the viewers."

"Sweet home Alabama
Where the skies are so blue ..."

When I finish the song, the host catches me off-guard by asking, "I hear someone in particular said you shouldn't be a singer, who was that?"

I blink, dumbstruck. I didn't know my family history would be brought up in front of millions of viewers and I stumble, "Oh lots of people have told me not to sing," I laugh weakly and look into the camera.

"Like who? Who made you feel bad about your singing?" he persists, "and because of this person, isn't it true you never sang in front of others for over thirty years?"

And I can't do it. I can't tattle, snitch, get back, get even, or make fun of my father. He has been in prison, lost jobs, lost businesses, had an affair, and moved ever downward while I have moved on.

"Oh, you know, family, friends, teachers, you name it!" I say and laugh some more.

My father never sees the show. He would not have enjoyed it in the least. He takes each of my victories and moments of success or happiness as direct assaults. I have violated the code of paternal hierarchy and he will never forgive me.

Consequently, I don't share with him much of what I do or have done, and try to keep my visits home short and our conversation sweet. He never asks me questions, I never offer more than small talk.

On one of my more recent visits, I'm sitting next to my father on a beige leather couch waiting for the DVD my mother put in to start. He is stretched out, feet on the coffee table, hands behind his head. If there was a cartoon caption above him it would say "Nothing you can say or show will impress me." I study him, bracing myself for an exchange I already know will be unpleasant. He has grown thin and brittle, like his opinions and prejudices.

"Wait until you see Ronda's speech," my mother gushes about a university commencement address I recently gave and which she attended. It's her idea to share the video with my father, "You won't believe it, 10,000 people in the stadium, she got a standing ovation from all of them." My mother is building this up too much, which means he will have to tear it down. And, right on cue, he says,

"They weren't giving an ovation, they were stampeding out to get a good seat at lunch."

Ha-ha ...

My father and mother didn't go to college. I am hugely thankful they sent me. I wanted to be an airline stewardess but my father forbid it, "It's just a flying waitress job. You're going to college, you'll meet a higher quality boy to marry." He filled out one application to the college he thought I should attend, took me to see it and although I balked, he dropped the application in the mailbox on campus and said, "You're going."

I took pride in being the first person in our family to finish college and graduated summa cum laude. I eventually went on to earn my masters and doctorate degrees and become a professor.

"I always thought you'd be a stand up comic, not a professor," my mother confessed on the day of my graduation.

"I always thought professors had to be smart," my father added.

It had not been a primrose path to standing at a podium addressing graduates and their families.

I worked my way through grad school dressed as a gorilla.

I started my own singing telegram company and called it Shenanigrams. Wearing a monkey suit and red tutu I performed birthday and anniversary songs in between going to classes.

> *"You wanted spice in life so baby, here I am,*
> *Your very own gorilla singing telegram ..."*

It took me eleven years to get my doctorate because I was working full time and raising two sons as a single parent. When I got my first tenure track position at a small university in Pennsylvania, my parents trekked out from California to pay me a visit. My father walked through the first house I had bought on my own, turned to me, and stated,

"Real professors, I mean good professors, teach at places like Harvard and Stanford, don't they?"

The DVD whirrs, the screen goes black and then blue...

I have no expectations that my father will enjoy the upcoming video of my speech anymore than he would have enjoyed my TV appearance so I gird my loins for the sucker punch I know will be coming.

The DVD flickers on with the caption "University Graduation Ceremony Highlights."

"Highlights? If these are the highlights, you will not be on this one, Ronda" my father quips, looking straight ahead at the screen.

The opening scene shows me sitting with about twenty other professors in full academic regalia. I am sitting on a folding metal chair. The same kind of folding metal chair I sat in as I waited out my *Lew King Rangers Show* audition. Then—and now—I look tiny, unsure, and very nervous.

"Ladies and gentlemen, honored guests, faculty, students and family members, we are proud to introduce our speaker today, Dr. Ronda Beaman. She is the top rated teacher at our university and has been recognized as the President's Teaching Scholar of the year. She has been named the National Education Association's first 'Art of Teaching' award winner. In addition, she was selected as Outstanding Graduate Student and her dissertation in education garnered the top prize for scholarly work at Arizona State University, where she graduated with high honors."

I am feeling sickly self-conscious and my head begins to throb. I try to poke fun at myself before he does and laugh nervously, saying,

"Ha-ha, great piece of creative writing, huh Daddy? Remember how you introduced me to that guy in your office who said, 'Ron, you didn't tell me you had a beautiful daughter,' and then you said, 'The beautiful one is at home, this is the oldest one.' That was funny ..." I am looking at him, smiling weakly.

He does not respond to or acknowledge my attempt to divert him from the awkward recitation of my resume as the emcee continues.

"Before entering academe, Dr. Beaman worked in television hosting a regional show, then turned her talents to public relations and marketing, eventually owning her own company. She is a published author, and travels internationally as a speaker and consultant.

"In her spare time," at this there is laughter from the audience, but none in front of the TV set, "Dr. Beaman is a fitness trainer and executive coach. Please join me in welcoming our speaker, Dr. Ronda Beaman."

The introduction seems déjà-vu-ish. Then it dawns on me, it is reminiscent of all those Girl Scout banquets so long ago,

"Award for Most Cookies Sold goes to ..."

"Award for Most Effective Patrol Leader goes to ..."

Hearing my introduction, sitting next to my father and struggling to tamp down all the raw emotion and ignore all the recriminating rubble of our relationship, I am struck with a blinding flash of the obvious.

The thing about badges, awards, and even introductions is they don't tell the whole story. A more truthful introduction would also state that I slept only four hours a night for decades, that my determination to amount to something cost me a marriage, and that I have fought my way through disfiguring cancer and multiple sclerosis.

Being meritorious, it seems from my introduction, means not admitting losses, only the gains, only the promotions, only the achievement. It means recognizing only half a story. And I wonder if my father would approve of me, or appreciate my journey a little, if he knew about the tough stuff, too.

I find I am embarrassed by the litany of "look at me" accomplishments I hear in my introduction. What seemed inspired at the time I was living it sounds insipid listed out loud. My introduction is clearly the introduction of someone who went to great lengths to impress somebody.

And that somebody is sitting next to me.

My father hasn't moved a muscle and is in the same position as when the video started. I am sitting to his right, so I can't see his face or read his mind. But, after all these years, and with his voice always in my head, I can guess. The caption bubble would now say "Those who can, do ... those who can't, become teachers ... like Ronda."

The sight of myself walking up to the podium after the agony of the audible introduction startles me even more. My academic gown is festooned with pins given to me from fraternities, sororities, various societies, student clubs, and organizations. I have handmade turquoise necklaces draped down the front of my maroon and blue velvet doctoral robes that are gifts from my Native American students. My specially ordered three-point cap from Oxford is at a jaunty angle just like ...

... like my Brownie beanie.

There is no denying it. The pins, the sash, the hat—the whole get up is just a more elaborate version of my Girl Scout uniform.

How have I not seen it? Scout or speaker, daughter or mother, student or teacher, I'm a grown up version of the girl who wanted to sing, dance, and sell cookies. I may be wearing a different hat and uniform, but I am still Little Miss Merit Badge.

Wait a minute. No one paved the way for me, handed me a silver spoon, or even a hand. I kept trying, losing, trying again, failing and flailing to be my best. I should be proud of what I have done, of who I have become ... he should be proud, I think, as I take a deep breath to calm down and try to enjoy watching the video, despite my father's feigned interest and cloying hostility.

I remain proud of myself for at least five more minutes more until the video ends with the promised 10,000 person, standing ovation. Instantly I blush and break into a discomforting sweat. Like a time traveler, I'm again the girl wearing the well-worn psychological kevlar sash of Girl Scout badges as I steel myself to look at my father. I begin a silent countdown waiting for him to launch the critique, cutting remark, or joke he will tell to leave me feeling wounded and inconsequential.

Five ... Four ... Three ... Two ...

Instead, I behold something akin to Halley's Comet, the Aurora Borealis and rain in the Gobi desert all in one fell swoop.

I see one tear drop from his right eye as he stares at the now blank and buzzing television screen. I watch it drip down his cheek, dropping onto his chest. I am unblinking and mesmerized, like a chemist studying a rare and previously unseen life form under the microscope, as I study the parsimonious fluid spreading on my father's cotton shirt. He doesn't look at me, but at last utters what has, until now, been our unspoken motto during all the years I tried Being My Best...

"I had no idea."

*... through storytelling and creative expression,
girls gain a better understanding of themselves and
their potential, and develop confidence to become
leaders in their own lives and in the world.*

GIRL SCOUT BADGE BOOK

Epilogue
The Journey Award

He used to wash my hair, I think as I stare at the water running down the hospital sink. The nurses are cleaning up and disinfecting the area where my father died only moments before. His life is literally going down the drain.

The scent of the eucalyptus shampoo floats back to me. I can see my eight-year-old self leaning over the bathroom sink, my father standing behind me. We are laughing. His fingers feel tender and strong as he suds through my hair.

You don't wash the head of a kid you don't love, I think, trying to amend the memory of our fractured relationship.

I leave the emergency room and walk toward the EXIT sign. Even though he didn't think I had any talent and he thought little of my achievements, he must have loved me in his own way.

My father is dead, I whisper trying it on. I let the words wash over me ... I feel not sadness exactly, but a grave sense of loss.

I have lost the chance to ask him ...

"Why?"

Why couldn't he have loved me more, listened to me with interest, or helped me find ways to believe in myself? Why could he not encourage me in my endeavors, or could it be that he believed his negativity and narcissism spurred me on to prove myself? And how can I be sure that it didn't?

Lost, too, is the opportunity to comprehend the source of his seething anger, who he blamed for his disappointments, and why he couldn't have cared enough about his family to have made even the smallest effort to be kind, or generous of spirit—as a rule, not an exception.

I mourn not for his passing, but for all the unanswered questions and squandered promises that are his deepest remains.

A few weeks after my father died, my mother held a life celebration in his honor. He had continued his peripatetic lifestyle, so the gathering was small, mostly current tennis buddies and his children. No one gave a eulogy and no one who was sober cried. There was a blurb in the tennis club newsletter that mentioned his death and his strong forehand.

That afternoon, sitting with my mother and siblings, we all

shared whatever warm stories we could dredge up about "Daddy."

"Remember when he said that Mother had her jeans custom made ... by Omar the tentmaker!"

"How about that time Daddy was driving and saw the black family who moved to our neighborhood crossing the street so he sped up to scare them!"

"Or when he asked Ronda why she exercises so much and she said she wanted to look as good as Jane Fonda when she's her age, and Daddy shot back, 'You don't look that good now.'"

Ah, the good old days.

My family continued their walk down memory lane. I listened and watched them, and I felt love for them. They were my first troop, after all, and had earned their own badges guided only by a generally harsh, unpleasant, and selfish leader.

And I loved my father, in a commandment kind of way.

But then my mother put the final nail in my coffin of fond memories when she turned to me, after telling a warm story of how my father had taken in a sick kitten at work, "Your father was nice to everyone ... except you." And with that she went to her room to lie down.

Family. The ties that bind ... and gag. The hairball I wanted to cough up kept me from thanking her for the Hallmark moment.

The next day she sent me home with a box of photos saying, "Daddy would want you to have these to remember him in better days."

Better days must mean before I was born, I thought, with a little too much self-pity.

And sure enough, these photos were of the better days, the days before he became our father. I find the famous yearbook shot of him in his letterman's jacket. There's also a school newspaper clipping about his high school fan club. Another photo shows him standing next to the Ford coupe he was given by his parents. I remember he told me that his name was engraved in silver on the dashboard. There are also photos of he and my mother on their way to the prom. They are young and lovely, with their full lives in front of them. And after that night my full life was in front of them, too.

As I rifle through the remaining glimpses into his young and once handsome life, a black and white picture that is slightly removed from and under the rest of the pile catches my eye. Like excavating through the rubble of a house fire, looking for any family jewels or precious mementos that have made it through the inferno, I pick through the other photos in the stack and carefully lift the small picture. I blink back instantaneous tears, the first I have cried since he died, not believing what I have salvaged.

It is a photo of my father as a boy, a duffle bag thrown over his shoulder ... wearing his Boy Scout uniform.

Why didn't, why wouldn't he tell me he was a scout? I wonder. Did he earn merit badges, too? Did he go to pack meetings? What about the oath? Did he take the oath? Didn't he believe it? What did I find in scouting for my life that eluded him?

I had no idea.

It's as if everyone is born with an empty sash, I think as I gather the scattered photos, and we each get to choose which badges we merit and which badges we rebuff due to lack of interest, desire, talent, or capability.

I discovered integrity, truth, hard work, goals, and commitment within the circle of each Girl Scout badge. But it is outside the circumference of the badges that I faced even more rigorous requirements; among them, forgiveness, compassion, love, courage, resilience, faith, and steadfast hope. I failed at these virtues more often than not, I often lost my way, and I sometimes celebrated mistaken victories. As a young girl I wasn't able to see beyond the badge. It took years to understand that I could never have what was inside each of them until I secured what lay outside of them. And what was outside those badges was not my father, my family, or any troop, what lay outside was my life.

I speak to the photograph of the dapper young stranger in the crisp and creased Boy Scout uniform, but am addressing my father,

"All this time the singing, the dancing, the trying out and getting in, the high degrees and multiple titles, the striving, thriving and achieving, the fighting back from failure, and the pursuit of possibilities ... I thought I was doing it for you. Now I know I was doing it so I could outgrow you. I did it so I could be a better, bigger version of myself than the one I saw reflected in your eyes."

I say an overdue and final "Good-bye," as I toss the photo back into the pile and put the lid on the box.

I shove the box into the back of a cupboard, close the door and walk away.

I feel prepared for my next journey, trusting that no matter where it leads, there will be merit.

Scout's honor.

Acknowledgements

What you leave behind is not what is engraved in stone monuments, but what is woven into the lives of others.

— PERICLES

"You lived it, why would you want to write about it?" The question came from others, as well as me on more than one occasion. As the "me"—which begins the word memoir—gets tiresome and necessarily narcissistic, I can only hope that my tale will empower others to keep trying, keep believing, and keep striving toward who and what they might become regardless of circumstance or capabilities. There may be errors in my re-telling, but the intent is honest.

My brother and sister have their own story; it is not mine to tell. I have tried respectfully to only give my version and leave the details and depth of their lives alone.

Thank you to my agent William Clark, your early belief in the work convinced me it had merit. Thanks, too to Jennifer Lauck, author of the memoir *Blackbird*, who gave my idea wings. I am grateful for my publisher Nancy Cleary, a fan of Girl Scout cookies, who saw the power in a simple story and my editor Tina Miller, who, after multiple readings, could have used a few boxes of Thin Mints herself.

It has been said you can't pick your family, but you get to pick your friends. I have made some excellent choices! I am indebted to Carol Lorek, Mary Kay Harrington, and Kim Scott, dear friends who were early readers and helped me shape the stories, Danielle Steussey who supported my vision with her graphic interpretations, and Jesse Dundon for his part in making The Merit Badge Project™ a reality.

Varian Ranch Boot Camp is the closet thing I will ever have to extended family. Working out with you, building cabins, hiking, hula hooping, eating, drinking, and being merry, it's like having lots of brothers and sisters, aunts and uncles, cousins, and nieces and nephews every time we are together. I love you guys.

My life has been deeply enriched by my students past and present, I am honored to be a small part of their lives. I am unable to name all of you who mean so much to me, but know you are being thanked for the vital part you have played in making my life so meaningful.

Special thanks to my STARS, particularly Lisa Gilbert Chrzanowski and Peggy Rittmann Vaughn for their support of anything and everything I do. I appreciate my assistant and former student, Arianna Spoto, for running my life, former students, and current public relations/marketing professionals Jennifer Masse and Natalie Beck for their talent and time, Caitlin Dooley and Odie Cawley for being my daughter wannabes and Colin Rizzo, limo driver and adopted son.

Speaking of sons and daughters, even the thesaurus lacks the right words to express my love, happiness, and pride in being the mother of Chase and Sean, did I really have a life before you? And daughter-in-law Katie, thank you for your kindness, full heart, and open love for our family, smartest thing I ever did was choose you!

And, PG ... my husband, best friend, and my home ... we are family, yesterday, now, and forever. I love you.

Book Club Questions

What was special or compelling about the context (time and place) or setting of *Little Miss Merit Badge*? What feelings, memories, thoughts did it evoke or trigger inside of you?

What specific themes did the author emphasize throughout her story? What do you think is her primary message to you, as her reader?

In what ways can you relate to Ronda and her challenges, her family and their predicaments? How did these remind you of yourself or someone you know?

How does Ronda—her character, perspective and sense of identity—change or evolve throughout the course of the story? What events were her key catalysts for change?

In what ways do the events and Ronda's reactions reveal evidence of her worldview? If you could put it in one sentence, how would you describe her worldview?

What parts of her story, if any, made you feel the most uncomfortable? Why?

By reading this book, what did you discover or re-discover about your self or your life?

What did you find most surprising, interesting, even disturbing about the adults depicted in *Little Miss Merit Badge*?

How has reading this book changed or enhanced your opinion of Girl Scouts? Teachers? Parenting?

To what extent does Ronda present her struggles in a way that is relatable and insightful? Specifically how does she do so?

How has *Little Miss Merit Badge* affected your perspective on the importance of forgiving those who hurt you, in order to move forward in life?

How has *Little Miss Merit Badge* helped you examine the role your parents played in your self-image or resilience?

For you, what is the "gem"—the key takeaway or lesson—you gained from this book?

Author Ronda Beaman looks forward to appearances at your book club meeting ... in person, by Skype, by phone, by Twitter! Please visit **www.LittleMissMeritBadge.com** for ideas and giveaways.

THE AUTHOR

Dr. Ronda Beaman still secretly believes The Beach Boys song was written for her. She is also a national thought leader for The American Health Network and her work has been featured on major media including *USA Today*, CBS, NBC and Fox.

Dr. Ronda is available to speak at troop meetings, book clubs and readings, writing seminars, and anywhere people gather to find humor, insights, and answers to life's most basic question, "When do I get my prize?"

Find her at **LittleMissMeritBadge.com**
littlemissmeritbadge@gmail.com

Earn badges of your own on her Facebook app
The Merit Badge Project.

CPSIA information can be obtained at www.ICGtesting.com
Printed in the USA
LVOW120358071211

258196LV00002B/3/P